THE
GREAT COMPOSERS
THEIR LIVES AND TIMES

Bedřich
Smetana
1824-1884

Antonín
Dvořák
1841-1904

Edvard
Grieg
1843-1907

Jean
Sibelius
1865-1957

THE GREAT COMPOSERS
THEIR LIVES AND TIMES

Bedřich

Smetana
1824-1884

Antonín

Dvořák
1841-1904

Edvard

Grieg
1843-1907

Jean

Sibelius
1865-1957

MARSHALL CAVENDISH
NEW YORK · LONDON · SYDNEY

Staff Credits

Editors
Laura Buller
David Buxton

Art Editors
Helen James
Debbie Jecock

Deputy Editor
Barbara Segall

Sub-editors
Geraldine Jones
Judy Oliver
Nigel Rodgers

Designers
Steve Chilcott
Shirin Patel
Chris Rathbone

Picture Researchers
Georgina Barker
Julia Calloway
Vanessa Cawley

Production Controllers
Deborah Cracknell
Sue Fuller

Secretary
Lynn Small

Publishing Director
Reg Wright

Managing Editor
Sue Lyon

Consultants
Dr Antony Hopkins
Commander of the Order
of the British Empire
Fellow of the
Royal College of Music

Nick Mapstone BA, MA

Keith Shadwick BA

Reference Edition Published 1990

Published by Marshall Cavendish Corporation
147 West Merrick Road
Freeport, Long Island
N.Y. 11520

Typeset by Maclink, Hull
Printed by Times Offset Private Ltd.,
Singapore

© *Marshall Cavendish Limited MCMLXXXIV,*
MCMLXXXVII, MCMXC

Library of Congress Cataloging-in-Publication Data

The Composers: the great composers, their lives and times.
  p. ca.
  Cover title: Great composers II.
  ISBN 1-85435-300-4 (set): $175.00
    1. Composers—Biography.   2. Music appreciation.
I. Marshall Cavendish Corporation.
II. Title: Great composers II.
ML390.C7185 1990   780'.92'2—dc20 [B]   89-23988

ISBN 1-85435-300-4 (set)   CIP
      1-85435-302-0 (vol)   MN

THE
GREAT COMPOSERS
THEIR LIVES AND TIMES

Contents

Introduction

In the mid-19th century, Europe underwent a radical change as a wave of political feeling swept throughout its individual countries. A new word, nationalism, was coined to describe this emotional movement; soon, nationalist elements began to appear in music. Under the influence of the Romantic movement, music prior to the 1850s showed a universality in style, but much written in the latter half of the century is clearly identifiable in terms of national origin. Nationalism – the awareness of the unique features of a nation, especially the rhythmic and melodic elements of its folk dance and music, and the desire to emphasize and glorify these elements – became the prominent movement in music. The four composers in this volume sought to express in their music national, rather than individual, identity, creating beautiful and enduring works.

Bedřich Smetana used the folk traditions of Czechoslovakia to great effect in his works. As the founder of the Czech national style in opera, he helped to break ground for other Bohemian composers. Antonín Dvořák responded to native traditions not only of Bohemia but also of America in his sweeping compositions. He became one of the first nationalist composers to find fame outside his own country. In Norway, Edvard Grieg followed the same nationalist goals as Smetana and Dvořák had. His works helped to unite and inspire Norwegians as their country moved toward independence. Finland's Jean Sibelius used Finnish legends to inspire his earlier works, but as his individual voice developed, his music began to reflect the transition between the Romantic nationalist era and the modern movement of the early twentieth century.

THE GREAT COMPOSERS

Bedřich Smetana

1824–1884

Bedřich Smetana established almost singlehandedly the national operatic tradition of Czechoslovakia. Like his younger contemporary, Antonín Dvořák, he sought influence in the folk traditions of his homeland; Smetana, however, concentrated on the rhythms and pacing of folk songs rather than on melody. He used national and patriotic themes to great effect, celebrating the country to whose artistic renaissance he had done much to create. The Moldau (Vltava), from his series of symphonic poems, Má Vlast, an affectionate portrait of the Vltava River, is examined in the Listener's Guide. *Dvořák also looked to Bohemia to influence his Cello Concerto in B minor, analysed in the* Listener's Guide. *Both these composers expressed their passionate love for a homeland which finally achieved independence in 1918, as detailed in* In The Background. *The appeal of their works, however, is international.*

Bedřich Smetana's compositions epitomized the spirit of a nation on the verge of independence. Born in Bohemia, he began to compose as a student, but financial difficulties forced him to open a piano school in Prague. He spoke German and composed in the German style, but while in Prague, he was encouraged to support the growing nationalist movement by becoming a truly Czech composer. It was a decision that was profoundly to shape his life. During the 1860s, he achieved national acclaim and also supported other Czech musicians by helping to establish a national opera house, where he was named director. The years of his directorship were not without controversy; some accused him of arrogance. His difficulties were compounded by the onset of deafness; by 1874 he was totally deaf. During his trying last years, Smetana completed Má Vlast among other memorable works, but due to physical ailments and frequent attacks of depression, he entered an asylum in Prague, where he died in 1884.

'My country'

**Although his younger contemporary Dvořák
achieved greater international fame, it is Bedřich
Smetana, the first Bohemian nationalist composer,
who is regarded as the founder of Czech music.**

Bedřich Smetana was the fore-runner of the composers who sought to express in their music the spirit and identity of the people and regions which were to become Czechoslovkia. Smetana originally worked in the German tradition and spoke German. Gradually he became aware of his true heritage and the rebirth of a national culture and a break from Austrian domination became his artistic goals.

Bedřich Smetana was born on 2 March 1824 in Litomyšl. He was the first son born to František Smetana, a brewer and his third wife Barbora Lyknová. František who was himself a very musical person hoped that his son would be a musician and gave the future composer his first music lessons when he was about four years old. By the time Bedřich was five he could play in quartets and soon he began taking lessons from a local musician, Jan Chmelík. Under Chmelík's guidance he blossomed as a performer and by the time he was six he had played as the soloist in a concert at the local Academy of Philosophy.

By 1825, the family now numbered eight children and larger premises were needed. In 1831 they

As students in Prague Smetana and his friends attended as many operas at the Theatre of the Estates (below) as their funds permitted.

moved to Jindřichuv Hradec in southern Bohemia, where Smetana's father took over the running of a brewery owned by Count Czernin. The count, who was a good violinist and the proud owner of a piano which had been played upon by Mozart, encouraged Smetana's musical development.

After his father's retirement in 1835 to a comfortable estate in south-east Bohemia, Bedřich had to attend a grammar school in Jihlava, 30 miles away from the new family home. He took weekly lodgings in the town, and despite the fact that there was an opera house in the town he was not happy there. With his brother Antonín he moved to a new school in Německý Brod where he was delighted to find that one of the teachers was a keen music-lover. This teacher introduced him to many of the popular opera composers of the day, such as Weber.

A student in Prague

By the time Smetana was 15 he wanted to get to Prague. With its German opera house and concert halls, which attracted musicians and singers from all over Europe, it was the cultural capital of Bohemia. He was sent to the Academic Gymnasium (high school) in Prague but he was so keen to savour all the artistic delights of the city, including a series of concerts by Liszt, that he spent much time playing truant

After a long courtship Smetana and Kateřina Kolářová (left) were married in 1849. Following the tragic death of three of their children Kateřina became ill with tuberculosis. She died on the return journey to Bohemia from Göteborg, Sweden (centre) where they had lived from 1856 until the spring of 1859.

from school. From 1840–3 he attended a school in Pilsen where there was not so much to distract him from his academic work. Despite his lack of formal training he had already composed a great deal of music for performance in local music circles. When his school days ended in 1843 he felt certain that his future was to be in music. He wrote in his diary: 'With God's help I shall equal Liszt in technique and Mozart in composition'.

His father, who had first encouraged his interest in music, supported him in his ambitions, but because of his own financial difficulties after retirement was only able to offer limited practical help. When Bedřich arrived back in Prague he found himself in a difficult situation. He was too old to join the Conservatory as a student and was unable to pay for private music lessons or even to hire a piano. To complicate matters, while he was in Pilsen he had fallen in love with a young pianist Kateřina Kolářová. However, he was in no position to pursue her and she did not fancy the idea of a penniless young musician as her suitor. His love for her found its expression in many piano pieces and eventually, after a long courtship, he persuaded her to marry him. Smetana did not allow his ambitions to be thwarted by these financial difficulties – he met and impressed the blind pianist Josef Proksch so much that he agreed to take him on as a pupil in musical theory at his own independent school of music.

In 1844 Smetana's luck changed and Jan B. Kittl, the director of the conservatory, hearing of his situation, found him a post as teacher to the family of Count Leopold Thun. He earned 300 gulden a year in the post, which he held until the summer of 1847.

All the while he took advantage of opportunities to widen his knowledge and appreciation of music. In 1846 Berlioz gave a series of concerts in Prague; Liszt made another visit followed by Robert and Clara Schumann. Through his music teacher Proksch, Smetana was given introductions to these famous musical people.

His musical studies over, Smetana, aged 23, decided to establish himself as a pianist. Kateřina took over

his post with Count Thun and he arranged a series of piano recitals in towns near to Prague. Sadly they were so poorly attended that he was forced to cancel the series.

In 1848 he applied for a licence to open a music teaching school. In an attempt to finance this he sent his Opus 1 – Six Characteristic Pieces – to Liszt (to whom they were also dedicated) asking his help in finding a publisher and requesting a loan of 400 gulden. Liszt ignored the request for money, but

In July 1860 Smetana married Bettina Ferdinandová (left). They had two daughters (above), Božena and Zdenka.

On his return to Prague in 1861 from a second trip to Sweden, where he tried to revive his failing fortunes, Smetana heard about an opera competition organized by Count Jan Harrach. The purpose of the competition was to establish a core of Czech opera. Smetana's entry was his first opera, The Brandenburgers in Bohemia *(the poster announcing it is shown above). First performed in January 1866, it was a great success and he was awarded the Harrach prize.*

wrote back to say he thought highly of the work and would do his best to find a publisher – the music was not in fact published until 1851.

Revolution and marriage

Smetana became aware, at this time, of his own potential role in the nationalist struggle. His uncle Professor František Smetana of Pilsen, an ardent believer in Czech independence, urged Smetana to support the cause and become a Czech musician rather than a German one. The decline of Metternich's powers in Austria gave the Czechs a feeling that the years of Austrian dominance might be ending. Revolution broke out in Prague on 11 June 1848.

Smetana joined the revolutionary forces and was inspired to write some marches and freedom songs for his compatriots. He also realized that if he was to fulfil his self-imposed task of becoming a Czech composer he would have to master the Czech language – he was not a natural linguist and it took him many years to break away from the use of German.

In the late summer of 1848 Smetana decided to take a risk and to open his own music school. Unfortunately it did not bring in as much money as he had hoped for, and once again he had to rely heavily on fees paid to him by private pupils from the noble families he had contacts with.

In August 1849 he at last persuaded Kateřina to marry him. Their first years were passed in great happiness. They made ends meet through teaching, and Smetana wrote much piano music, dances and a symphony. Before long their happiness was clouded by the deaths of three of their four daughters between 1854–55 and Kateřina herself became ill with tuberculosis.

In the aftermath of the revolution of 1848 many of its supporters felt that it would be safer to quit Prague. Smetana decided to seek musical opportunities in Sweden and together with Kateriná and their surviving daughter travelled to Göteborg, arriving in September 1856.

Exile in Sweden

In Sweden Smetana was comparatively successful. He gave his first well-received concert in Göteborg soon after he arrived; this was followed by many such performances and in December 1856 he opened a music school. He also became conductor of the local choral society, which seemed to flourish under his direction. He acquired many rich pupils and in 1857 prepared a series of important chamber recitals and choral concerts. Socially life in Göteborg was pleasant, and despite the fact that he found its artistic life unbearably conservative, he did seriously consider living there permanently.

In the summer of 1857, just before his father's death he returned to Prague. After the funeral he made the journey back to Sweden with his wife and one surviving daughter, calling on Liszt in Weimar on the way. There he met the conductor Johann Herbeck who did Czech music a great service by telling Smetana that in his opinion the Czechs were nothing more than a race of fiddlers, totally unable to produce one composer with a national identity. Liszt defended Smetana and played the opus 1 music to Herbeck. The challenge was enough however, to make Smetana vow to devote his life to the creation of a true Czech music.

In the spring of 1859, Smetana felt that although Kateřina was still ill, it would be better for her to be in her homeland with friends and family, so they set off to return to Bohemia. En route, in Dresden, Kateřina became seriously ill and she died there on 19 April 1859.

To occupy his mind and assuage his grief Smetana

was produced in January 1866, it was a great success – and Smetana was awarded the Harrach prize. His second opera, *The Bartered Bride,* was put into production in May 1866 at the Provisional Theatre but probably because of the political conditions – the Austro-Prussian war was imminent – it didn't meet with instant success. After five separate revisions, it was revived in September 1870 and was triumphantly received.

In the meantime after his success with *The Brandenburgers in Bohemia,* Smetana had been appointed principal music director at the Provisional Theatre – a post which he held for the next eight years.

As musical director Smetana counter-balanced his predecessor Mayr's leanings towards Italian opera. It

Smetana's second opera **The Bartered Bride** *(the set and costume designs shown left and above were for a 1928 production) was very light-hearted in comparison to* **The Brandenburgers in Bohemia.** *On its first performance in May 1866 it met with only mild success, but its revival in 1870 was a triumph. Smetana was honoured with a banquet after its 100th performance in 1882.*

immersed himself in music and musical politics. At Liszt's invitation he went to Leipzig where among many new musical experiences he heard Wagner's *Tristan und Isolde* for the first time. On his return to Bohemia later that year he became engaged to Bettina Ferdinandova, a relative by marriage. In September he returned to Göteborg where he once again busied himself composing and giving recitals.

After his marriage to Bettina in July 1860 he decided that after the winter season in Göteborg he would return again to Bohemia from his self-imposed exile. He at last returned to Prague in May 1861.

Back to Bohemia
His first ventures on his return to Prague in May 1861 were not financially successful. Bitterly disappointed with the poor response to his concert tours of Germany and Holland and a series of concerts in Prague, Smetana made one more trip to Göteborg to earn enough money to keep him going.

When he returned to Prague Smetana heard that the newly opened Provisional Theatre intended to encourage the production of opera. Count Harrach, a Czech patriot and Chairman of the Building Committee for the National Theatre, had offered two prizes of 600 gulden for the best operas written on Czech subjects. Until this point Smetana had not been much attracted to opera, but he decided to take this opportunity to compose in this genre.

He entered his first opera, *The Brandenburgers in Bohemia,* for the competition, and although there were many obstacles and disappointments before it

Smetana (centre) and Antonín Dvořák (third from the left in second row) are regarded as the pillars of Czech nationalist music. Their paths first crossed in 1866 when Smetana was conductor of the Provisional Theatre Orchestra. At that time Dvořák was a viola player in the orchestra. The age and language differences between them probably made friendship unlikely, but each held the other's music in high esteem.

The Kiss (title page above), completed in 1876, was one of Smetana's most popular operas.

The National Theatre (above, from a newspaper report) was re-opened in May 1883 with a performance of one of Smetana's earlier operas, Libuše.

from its ranks of skilled and professional musicians that the nucleus of the Provisional Theatre Orchestra was drawn. When Smetana became conductor of the Provisional Theatre Orchestra in 1866 Dvořák was a viola player in the orchestra. Smetana was fast gaining a reputation as the leader of Czech music, and although it is likely that age and language differences between the two made friendship unlikely, there is no doubt that Dvořák gained much encouragement for his own operatic ambitions.

In 1871 Dvořák himself submitted an opera to the Provisional Theatre. Smetana conducted the overture at a concert but that was as far as it got for the time being. Smetana's view of it was that it was 'a serious work, full of genius, but unperformable'. The opera – *King and Collier* – disappeared. Dvořák re-wrote the score but it was not actually performed until 1929.

In order to realize his ambitions of popularity outside Bohemia, Smetana chose for his next opera a German text, *Dalibor,* which was also translated into Czech for home production. It was finished by 1867 and performed on the day of the laying of the foundation stone of a new and permanent National Theatre in Prague on 16 May 1868. On this memorable day Smetana, along with other men in the forefront of Czech artistic life, took part in the ceremony. As he helped to set the stone in position he solemnly declared that music was the lifeblood of the Czechs.

was at this point that the young composer Dvořák came into the same musical arena as Smetana. Dvořák's first musical job was in an orchestra conducted by Karel Komsák. Komsák himself was a composer of light music and his orchestra generally played this as well as a mixture of popular overtures, marches and dances in the Prague restaurants and dance-halls. Although lightweight in output it was

Criticism and illness

Despite his hard work for Czech music, some contemporaries accused Smetana of Wagnerian tendencies, and when the light-hearted *The Bartered Bride* was played again in 1871 it was criticized for being too much like the frivolous work of Offenbach. Smetana was deeply hurt by these accusations and he was also running into trouble at the theatre where

Prague (right) had always fascinated Smetana and in his last years it gave him great pleasure just to be there. His visits to Prague from the countryside around Jabkenice where he lived with his married daughter seemed to give him consolation and he always returned revitalized.

his musical directorship was unpopular with some members of the board. Their efforts to dismiss him were counteracted by a petition from the musicians who admired his work – Dvořák among them. His appointment was re-confirmed at the beginning of 1873 with an increased salary.

An all-out attack by his enemies continued and a sharp exchange between Smetana and Mayr built up to a climax. Mayr accused Smetana of arrogance in meddling with other people's scores. Many of his critics accused him of undermining the cause of Czech opera by his Wagnerism. At about this time his health began to deteriorate. In April 1874 he recorded that he was suffering from an ulcer, and later that he had a throat infection and an irritating body rash. This was followed by giddiness which was attributed to a blockage in the ears. By September 1874 Smetana had to face the tragedy that had assailed Beethoven before him – he was on the verge of deafness. He wrote to tell his theatre committee that he was totally deaf in his right ear and the left one was failing rapidly. He complained of a continual noise like a waterfall that confused everything for him. The doctor managed to give him some relief through treatment but by November he was totally deaf and the incessant noise in his ears was driving him to the verge of madness. His critics – unrelenting – continued to assail him on all sides. He found consolation at this time by starting to compose the cycle of symphonic poems that make up *Má Vlast* (My Country).

By 1876 he had completed another opera *The Kiss.* He had accepted the libretto with reluctance at first but soon fell in love with it and when the work was first performed in November 1876 it proved to be a great public triumph.

There was a new difficulty when the Theatre held up his salary and left him penniless. When his contract was renewed it was on the basis of his operas being performed without royalty there. Due to his financial situation he was forced to leave his Prague flat and with his family move to the home at Jabkenice of his daughter from his first marriage. His relationship with his second wife, already under some strain, deteriorated even further and in his dementia he accused her of all sorts of crimes.

The next opera to be completed was *The Secret* which was performed on 18 September 1878 to general acclaim. The last two movements of *Má Vlast–Tabor* and *Blanik* – were completed at the end of the year and performed at a special concert in his honour at the beginning of 1880. Of *Tabor* he said that it 'signified the fervour of faith'. 'Believe me,' he wrote to a friend, 'I need all my courage to keep myself from becoming desperate enough to end my life. Only my family and the thought of working for my country and my people keeps me alive and creative.'

Although there were still difficulties and disappointments in the staging of some of his new work, his older operas like *The Bartered Bride* continued to be favourites. In May 1882 following the 100th performance of *The Bartered Bride,* there were presentations and congratulations.

Public recognition

But even though his public was giving him the treatment he well-deserved, by the autumn of 1882 his physical suffering was even greater. His voice, which he had used at shouting pitch since his deafness, went altogether and he lost his memory. Despite these continuing afflictions, attributed now to the syphilis from which he suffered, he completed his Second String Quartet and several other works. On 18 November 1882 the rebuilt National Theatre was re-opened and Smetana's *Libuše* was chosen for the occasion. By April 1884 his mind was totally deranged and probably out of consideration for the safety of his family, his doctors committed him to the Prague lunatic asylum where he died on 12 May 1884. Three days later his funeral cortège made its way past the National Theatre to the Vysegrad Cemetery where he was buried.

In his old age and illness Smetana (above) was a sad figure. His friends noted that even in hot weather he wore a fur-trimmed coat. He died on 12 May 1884 in the Prague Lunatic Asylum. His funeral cortège (below) as a mark of respect took him past the National Theatre which he helped establish.

Czech orchestral works

Dvořák's towering B minor Cello Concerto **and Smetana's affectionate symphonic portrait** Vltava **were both inspired by the composers' native Bohemia – their appeal, however, is international.**

Dvořák: Cello Concerto in B minor, op. 104

Dvořák's first sojourn in America began in September 1892, a visit full of promise and high expectation. It proved to be a thoroughly productive time, for in that first season, during vacations from his teaching duties at the National Conservatory in New York, Dvořák wrote several of his most popular works – the 'New World' Symphony among them.

Yet, like most Czechs, Dvořák was desperately homesick, even when among the Bohemian emigrés with whom he spent his first summer at Spillville, Iowa. And when he did return home it was with considerable reluctance that he agreed to go back to New York for a further six months. This reluctance was not entirely due to homesickness however; it seems that his employer, the redoubtable Mrs Thurber, was rather less good at paying the composer's salary than at persuading him to work for her. She wanted him to stay on at the Conservatory for another year or two but he remained equivocal while she, in the meantime, produced endless excuses for being temporarily unable to pay him. In the end, the resourceful Mrs Thurber tried to pre-empt the situation by announcing that Dvořák had agreed to return.

In the circumstances it is perhaps scarcely surprising that Dvořák's enthusiasm for America was cooler the second time around. He arrived in New York in September 1894 and was forced to spend the entire winter season there. It was during November of that year that he began work on the Cello Concerto in B minor, the last composition he completed in America.

Whereas the 'New World' Symphony – with its fleeting references to plantation music and Indian folk song – had contained elements of a native American music Dvořák's Cello Concerto looks back nostalgically to Bohemia, and specifically to the country estate at Vysoká where he lived. His Cello Concerto belongs there entirely and hints at nothing that could be termed 'American'.

It was not the first cello concerto Dvořák had written, but he had always considered

Dvořák had grave misgivings about the suitability of the cello as a solo instrument – it would not, he felt, be able to hold its own against an orchestra. Happily, he was persuaded to change his mind – many think by his cellist friend Hanuš Wihan (above) to whom the Cello Concerto in B minor is dedicated. Dvořák wrote the work during his second tour of America, but it has little to do with the 'new world'. It looks back nostalgically to his native Bohemia (left).

In the second and third movements, Dvořák quotes from an earlier work, his Four Songs op. 82 (title page right). One of the songs 'Leave me alone' had been a particular favourite of Josephina Kaunitzova, with whom Dvořák had been in love. She is pictured above with her sister Anna who later became the composer's wife.

its predecessor, composed at the beginning of his career, a failure. (He never orchestrated the piece, and it was not published in orchestral form until 1929.) This early attempt had convinced Dvořák that, although the cello had a notable place in chamber and orchestral music, it was not cut out to be a soloist since it was incapable of holding its own against a modern symphony orchestra. Nor was its 'nasal' upper register or its rumbling bass much to his taste either.

So what made him change his mind? Some say that his friend Hanuš Wihan, cellist with the Bohemian Quartet, persuaded him to write another concerto for the instrument; others maintain that, on hearing the first performance in New York of his friend Victor Herbert's Second Cello Concerto, he was awakened to the possibility of composing a great concerto

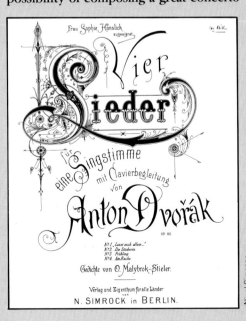

of his own. Herbert, now better remembered as the author of operettas and musical comedies, surely had some influence on Dvořák. His concerto employed some unusual features, notably three trombones, which if Dvořák's fears had any foundation, should have swamped the luckless soloist. The editor of the latest edition of Dvořák's score does not acknowledge any debt to Herbert. Nevertheless, for the first time in his concertos Dvořák abandoned the strictly 'classical' orchestra in favour of one which incorporated not only Herbert's three trombones, but a tuba and, in the finale, a triangle as well.

Once started, Dvořák's progress was steady and orderly. He sketched the movements in a small notebook, scoring each one as he went along. The first movement, begun on 8 November 1894, was completed in score by 12 December. The second appears to have followed at once and was finished on 30 December. The last movement, to quote the composer, 'begun at the New Year' was completed on 9 February, though not in its final form. It was in this form however that Dvořák took the concerto back home with him when he left America for the last time in April 1895.

A change of heart

The revisions Dvořák made after his return to Vysoká were important, not just for musical reasons but for personal ones. On the manuscript score the composer wrote: 'I finished the concerto in New York, but when I returned to Bohemia, I changed the end completely as it stands here now. Pisek 11.6.1895.' During that summer he prepared the piano score which he completed on 25 September.

As with all great works of art there is more to this concerto than is apparent at a casual first glance. We know that Dvořák conceived the work in a nostalgic frame of mind: Bohemia conjured it into being, whatever stimulated its actual composition. Virtually everything about it – its melodies, rhythms and colour – is Bohemian, but there is a tragically autobiographical element in it too. Knowing about it, however, is not essential to our enjoyment of the music. Brahms, for example, was unaware of any personal element, yet Brahms realized that his friend had produced an outstanding masterpiece in a notoriously difficult medium. In spite of having recently completed his own Double Concerto, op. 102 in which the cello plays the lion role, he grumbled good-naturedly 'Why did nobody tell me it was possible to write a cello concerto like this?'

Whatever its purely musical virtues, this concerto had more than ordinary importance for Dvořák, and he admitted as much. He dedicated the work to Hanuš Wihan and, despite a serious professional disagreement, the dedication remained (a

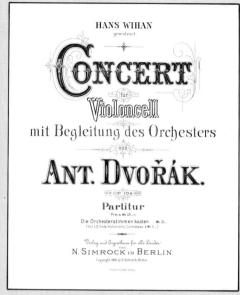

Although Dvořák and Wihan disagreed about the work, the title page of the Cello Concerto (above) retains the dedication to the cellist.

last movement . . . There is no cadenza in the last movement either in the score or in the piano arrangement. I told Wihan straightaway when he showed it to me that it was impossible to stick bits on like that. The finale closes gradually diminuendo, like a sigh – with reminiscences of the first and second movements – the solo dies down to pianissimo – then swells again and the last bars are taken up by the orchestra and the whole concludes in stormy mood. That was my idea and I cannot depart from it . . .

It has been supposed that Wihan did not give the first performance of the concerto as a result of this difference of opinion, but new evidence suggests otherwise. The première was to have taken place in London under the composer's direction with Wihan as soloist, but the cellist was unable to be present on the day. At first Dvořák was reluctant to keep the date himself, but when told by the Philharmonic Society that it would be a considerable inconvenience if the concert were cancelled, he agreed to conduct. The soloist was an English cellist, Leo Stern, who gave the première at the old Queen's Hall on 19 March 1896. Stern was again the soloist when the concerto was first played in Prague by the National Theatre Orchestra (now the Czech Philharmonic) on 11 April. Wihan performed it for the first time in public in the Netherlands in 1899.

So what was the sacred ground that Wihan unconsciously violated with his cadenza? It concerned a lady, Dvořák's sister-in-law Josephina Kaunitzova. Dvořák had given piano lessons to Josephina back in 1862 when he was 21 and she an actress of 16. He had fallen

While working on the second movement Dvořák learned that Josephina was dying. The soulful mood of her favourite song, to which he refers, is reflected in Wasnjezow's painting (above).

testimony to the composer's basic generosity). Dedicatees, particularly of concertos, tend to be people who know a great deal about their art, and sometimes think they know as much about everyone else's – it is an attitude which is inclined to damage friendships.

In Dvořák's case it was Wihan's urge to insert a cadenza into the last movement at a point where Dvořák felt one to be unnecessary and unacceptable that caused the breach. Having taken advice from Wihan about a number of minor points the composer stuck fast when it came to what he regarded as a major issue. Occasionally the instinct to reject advice is ill-judged,

but not in this case. Wihan had quite unwittingly attempted to trespass on a sacred area of the concerto, and by trying to insert his own rhetorical commentary at that point, had earned for himself a more stinging rebuff than Dvořák's refusal to have a cadenza, any cadenza, strictly merited.

In his usual forthright manner Dvořák wrote to his German publisher Simrock in October 1895 saying, among other things:

I do not agree with my friend Wihan in regard to a number of places. I do not like many of the passages – and I must insist on my work being printed as I have written it. I shall only then give you my work if you promise not to allow anybody to make changes – my friend Wihan not excepted – without my knowledge and consent, and also not the cadenza which Wihan has added to the

desperately in love with her, and had written the songs *Cypresses* for her in a vain attempt to win her heart, but he eventually married her sister instead. News came to him in America while he was working on the second movement of the Cello Concerto that Josephina was seriously ill. In a melancholy mood, he introduced into the music (at bar 42) a modified reference to one of her favourite songs *Kéž duch můj sám* (Leave me alone), the first of his own Four Songs, op. 82, published in 1889. Josephina died on 27 May 1895, a few months after Dvořák's return from America, and it was this event that prompted him to make the drastic changes to the end of the last movement to which he refers on the manuscript score. As an intensely personal memorial to her, he replaced eight bars of music with sixty new ones based on his sister-in-law's favourite song. It was into this hallowed area of memory that Wihan sought to insert his virtuoso cadenza.

Programme notes

In writing a cello concerto, Dvořák was faced with the perennial problems of balance. As this was not intended as a virtuoso's showpiece in the manner of Paganini or Wieniawski, the soloist had to be integrated into the orchestral texture, but not so completely that he disappeared into it as if it were a sinfonia concertante. Also there was a danger of turning the opening orchestral introduction, the *tutti,* into something like the beginning of a symphony, in which case it would be difficult to get the soloist started except in a new key. In fact Dvořák almost fell into this last trap, but he solved the first problem – that of balance – admirably.

The Cello Concerto is unmistakably Bohemian in flavour. Like Smetana, Dvořák drew heavily on the folk dances of his homeland (below).

Jean-Loup Charmet

Understanding music: the influence of folk music

The influence of folk music is often most noticeable in the music of composers who have been associated with the gathering of folk tunes. Haydn, who lived in the borderland of Austria near Hungary and who may well have been a collector of folk tunes, subtly blended Croat and Magyar melodies into at least two of his symphonies – nos. 103 and 104, as well as into other works. However, the settings of British folksongs by Haydn and Beethoven, both commissioned by George Thomson, a collector of folk song, were in a musical idiom quite unrelated to the original folk songs. Liszt and Brahms both confused gypsy music with true Hungarian folk music and adapted the former to produce 'Hungarian' effects in their Hungarian Rhapsodies and Hungarian Dances, respectively. Dvořák, known to be interested in a wide range of folk music (while in the United States, he was introduced to Negro folk songs by the singer, Harry Burleigh) was influenced by folk music in his compositions, such as the *Slavonic Rhapsodies,* although he rarely quoted actual folk tunes.

Folk music in art music

Folk music has been incorporated into art music in a variety of ways. The rhapsody is a musical form commonly used to present folk tunes in original compositions. In addition to those by Liszt and Dvořák rhapsodies inspired by native or foreign folk music have been composed by the Frenchman, Edouard Lalo – his *Rhapsodie Norvegienne* is an affectionate and exhilarating acount of his impressions of Norwegian folk music; while Vaughan Williams wrote his *Norfolk Rhapsody* based on folk songs collected in that region and Delius's *Brigg Fair* is subtitled, 'An English Rhapsody'.

Inclusion of recognizable folk tunes in art music is also a common device. Saint-Saëns quotes a Tunisian folk tune in his *Africa,* op. 89, while the Mexican composer, Carlos Chávez (1899–1978) includes a Yacqui Indian folk tune in *Sinfonia India* – a piece, which in common with *Little Train of the Caipira* by the Brazilian, Villa-Lobos (1887–1959), is scored for a conventional orchestra augmented by native folk instruments.

Well before 'nationalist' composers began to include exotic folk instruments in their orchestration, the novelty of rustic instruments was imitated by earlier composers. Thus, in his *Musettes de Choisis et de Taverni,*

François Couperin mimicked the French bagpipe.

Recording folk music

In 1889, the year the Eiffel Tower was completed, Edison marketed his sound recording phonograph. A year later, another American, J. W. Fewkes used the phonograph to record performances of folk music. Six years later, the Hungarian, Béla Vikar and then in 1906, his compatriots, Bartók and Zoltan Kodály (1882–1967) began to use the phonograph as part of the systematic study and collection of folk music in Hungary and further afield. At this time, there was an awareness among these composers and others – Vaughan Williams, George Butterworth (1885–1916) and Holst, all involved in collecting folk music in Britain – of the impending decline and disappearance of folk music. All of these composers, including Mussorgsky and the Czech, Leoš Janáček (1854–1928), shared the view that folk tunes should not be patched on to classical compositions but should themselves provide the basis for new compositional forms.

The impact of folk music on modern music

Bartók's use of folk music he had collected became increasingly more sophisticated. At first, he wrote settings of folk tunes with minimal or no alteration of the original tunes as in his *Three Hungarian Folk Songs* for piano solo. Later, his compositions included very ingenious interweavings of elements of actual folk tunes with original composition based on the musical, and also the performance characteristics as recorded on phonograph cylinders of folk tunes – e.g. the two *Rhapsodies for Violin and Piano* – pieces which Bartók may have intended as trail blazers for his more abstract works to come. Although Bartók's friend Kodály was more conservative in his use of folk music as can be compared with his settings of folk songs in 'Hary Janos' and in 'Nine Pieces for Piano', op. 3, he too developed innovations in compositional structure.

In the twentieth century, elements of folk music – especially rhythm – have very much dominated the nature of art music. Increasingly after Bartók and Stravinsky, composers used folk music not only to produce exotic sounds in their works but also because its structural and harmonic differences have provided the foundations for new adventures in musical composition.

Julius Mařák 'On the verge of the Forest'. The National Gallery, Prague

in the lowest strings, and after four bars the first theme appears on the horns, to be taken up immediately by oboes and clarinets. This is to be the first of many ideas in this incredibly inventive movement. After a short orchestral climax the soloist introduces yet another theme and the movement unfolds in a mood of subdued reflection rather than as a dramatic dialogue. The key moves from B minor (the tonic) into B major and a long series of trills on B in the upper register of the cello heralds the approach of the coda. Josephina's song (Example 2a) is now heard as a soulful violin solo, and there are shadowy memories of the first movement too. Now Dvořák gives full reign to his grief and anguish. At length, he shakes himself free of his reminiscences and brings the concerto to a storming close.

Smetana: The Moldau (Vltava)

Rivers, particularly those which flow through great cities, acquire a personality of their own, and often find themselves celebrated in legend and song – the Thames, the Danube, Volga and Mississippi. But few have acquired such an

The last movement unfolds in a mood of subdued reflection (above) before Dvořák brings the Concerto to a brilliant end.

First movement: Allegro

The work opens in a surprisingly gentle fashion. There are none of the bravura flourishes one associates with the virtuoso concertos of the period, and the first theme (Example 1) is introduced by the clarinets over a quiet accompaniment in the lower strings.

Example 1

(musical notation)

It is echoed and extended by the first violins and oboes, quickly building towards a grand orchestral climax. Now, the second subject, in D major, is introduced by the horns. It is typical of Dvořák, a broad lyrical melody of great beauty, not especially passionate but redolent of all that is loveliest in the Czech landscape. With a subtle touch of genius he adds a little 'tail' to this tune in the form of an interplay between the woodwinds. Another orchestral *tutti,* on a new idea which is never to re-appear, successfully gets the soloist on stage in the home key. The cello enters *quasi improvisando* (in the manner of an improvization), and in a series of skilful variations begins to explore the opening theme (Example 1).

Now comes the development section of

this long yet concentrated first movement, sprouting much rich invention as it makes its way, via a distant key (A flat minor) towards the home key of B minor, but not, as might be expected, with a return to the opening material. Instead, Dvořák treats us to the second subject, now in the gorgeous regalia of the full orchestra, announced by a portentous drum roll and a scurrying upward-rising passage in octaves on the cello.

Second movement: Adagio, ma non troppo

The slow movement, in a moderately slow tempo, begins with another typically Dvořákian theme – a gentle, song-like tune. The key signature (two flats) suggests G minor, but the movement actually begins on the major, the introduction of the minor tonality being held in reserve until after the stormy orchestral climax. This prepares the ground for the cellist's first reference to Josephina's song (Example 2b):

Example 2
Song: 'Leave me alone'

Concerto

(musical notation)

The composer develops this theme with great feeling and at some length, finally returning to a greatly modified version of the opening material.

Third movement: Finale. Allegro moderato

The finale opens quietly, almost on tiptoe,

With the set of six symphonic poems, Má Vlast, Smetana set out to celebrate the spirit of his native country. The best known of the set, Vltava, is a brilliant musical portrait of the river which flows through the composer's beloved Prague (right).

Archiv für Kunst und Geschichte

encrustation of myth, legend and history as the great river that flows through Prague, and enshrines the spirit of the Czech Lands, the area of Czechoslovakia known more familiarly as Bohemia.

When, in 1874, the deaf and disillusioned Smetana, deprived of most of his livelihood by jealous rivalry and the onset of illness, set out to celebrate in music the country to whose artistic renaissance he had devoted so much of his life, he chose to do so in the form of a series of six symphonic poems. *Má Vlast* (My Country) covers a vast range of moods celebrating almost every aspect of Czech legend, history and landscape. It was inevitable therefore, that part of this celebration must include the river that Prague had taken to its heart.

Programme notes

All rivers rise somewhere, and Smetana depicts the sources (there are two) of the Vltava at the very outset – one a dripping, the other a rippling stream. These soon combine and broaden out. The river now passes through forest lands in which huntsmen gaily pursue their quarry, identified by typical hunting-horn calls.

On muted strings and in the mysterious key of A flat, Smetana depicts the water nymphs as they appear with the rising of the moon (left).

Carl Spitzweg 'Bathing Nymphs'. Private Collection. Joachim Blauel/Artothek

The river flows on to a village where a rustic wedding is taking place, and the tempo of the music changes from its initial 6/8 to a jolly dance in 2/4 time which, having run its course, fades as the Vltava wends its way through the twilight.

With the rise of the moon, the water nymphs appear and in another change of tempo and with the key moving from a bright G major to a mysterious A flat, they dance to a muted string accompaniment. The main Vltava theme (Example 3) reasserts itself as the river again takes the centre stage:

Example 3

The broad sweep of the stream quickens and then breaks up as the St John's Rapids throw the waters (and all the musical themes) into turmoil. Once passed, the river and music flow on. Now in full orchestral splendour the rivers salutes Prague in triumph, as it sweeps majestically by, then fades gradually away.

Soon the flow of the river quickens and breaks up as rapids throw the waters – and the musical themes – into tumbling confusion (left).

Hans Thoma 'The Rhein at Laufenburg'. Archiv für Kunst und Geschichte

Smetana brings the symphonic poem to a majestic conclusion as, in full dignity, the river sweeps onward and winds out of sight.

Frederick Sandys 'Whittingham, Autumn'. Christie's, London/The Bridgeman Art Library

Great interpreters

Godfrey MacDornnic

S. Lauterwasser/Deutsche Grammophon Production

George Szell (above left) the conductor and (right) the soloist, Pierre Fournier.

George Szell (conductor)
Biographical notes appear on page 101.

Pierre Fournier (cellist)
Pierre Fournier was born in Paris in 1906 into a musical family. His brother, Jean, went on to become a fine violinist. Pierre studied the piano with his mother but suffered from an attack of polio when he was nine years old. Determined to continue with music, he took up the cello and entered the Conservatoire, where he was taught by Paul Bazelaire and André Hekking. By the mid-20s he was establishing a reputation for himself in concerts throughout Paris, and in 1925 he participated in the first performance of Fauré's String Quartet.

International reputation
He pursued a successful chamber and solo career into the 1930s, and from 1937–39 was engaged as a teacher at the Ecole Normale de Musique. Two years later, during the German occupation, he taught at the Conservatoire itself, remaining there until 1943. That year he took Pablo Casals's place in the legendary trio with Thibaud and Cortot, and his reputation quickly spread internationally. After the war, he began touring Europe in earnest, often in tandem with such greats as the violinist Szigeti and the pianist Schnabel.

In 1948 he made his first tour of the USA. The Americans welcomed him enthusiastically, and during the next two decades he travelled there many times, recording as well as performing.

Fournier continued to perform well into his 70s, and has made many fine recordings at all stages of his career, both in the orchestral and chamber repertoire. He has a wonderfully assured, liquid technique and a very smooth tone. His tastes are broad and he has been a great advocate of modern music. In 1963 he was appointed Officer of the Legion d'Honneur.

FURTHER LISTENING

Smetana
Wallenstein's Camp
This overture shows how vividly Smetana could conjure up a complete picture of a place and an event. Based on a scene from Schiller's *Wallenstein* tragedy, the Czech setting, with soldiers moving off in a colourful procession, stimulated the composer to produce some of his most evocative music. The work is like a miniature symphony in four parts.

The Bartered Bride
Smetana's importance as a composer of opera has often been overlooked, and only *The Bartered Bride* has made a really deep impression on Western European audiences. The reason is not hard to find – the *Bride* is an essentially comic opera, full of high spirits and well-rounded characters. It broke new ground in its day, dealing as it does with ordinary country folk and provincial customs. Like Mozart's *Figaro,* it also has an underlying seriousness and several pointed comments to make. These help produce the tensions in the plot, which make it so successful dramatically.

Dvořák
Violin Concerto, op. 53
This, Dvořák's only other string concerto, is rich in bold, folk-inspired ideas, contained within a strong and vigorous thematic structure. The composer's deep attachment to the singing qualities of his country's folk music gave him a natural affinity for the violin, and accordingly he gives the soloist a continual stream of arresting and graceful melodies, both in the Adagio and the brilliant finale.

IN THE BACKGROUND

'Slava's daughter'

*Inspired by the music of their native Bohemia,
Dvořák and Smetana's work was celebrated as part
of a national revival that led to the establishment of
an independent Czechoslovak state.*

After the French Revolution and the Napoleonic Wars, the idea of the nation-state began to sweep through all the peoples of Europe. For the Slav peoples living in Central, Eastern and Southern Europe the idea of self-determination and independence was particularly compelling because – apart from Russia and the tiny state of Montenegro, jealously guarding its freedom among the most inaccessible Balkan mountains – they were all under non-Slav rule. So the Balkan Slavs groaned under the Turkish yoke and though the Slavs within the Austro-Hungarian Empire considered themselves lucky to be the subjects of the relatively enlightened Hapsburgs, they too were beginning to be conscious of political oppression.

Ironically, these 'Austrian Slavs', particularly the Czechs and the Slovaks, woke up to a sense of injured national pride just as their lot had begun to improve. Under the enlightened despotism of the Empress Maria Theresa (1740-80) and her son Joseph II (d. 1790), who reigned with and after her, great reforms were initiated throughout the vast Hapsburg realms. These changes included the freeing of peasant serfs, the provision of public educational opportunities and a new liberal legal code, which clearly defined the rights and duties of their Slav subjects. But, in practice, reform often meant Germanization, for in order to centralize and simplify the administration of their unwieldy, multi-lingual empire the Hapsburgs imposed German as the official language, thus trampling on emergent nationalist feelings among the Slavs.

But soon there were great economic compensations. The Napoleonic blockade (which prevented the British from trading with the Continent) gave a great boost to the Czech textile industry, and a new iron and steel industry, based on local coal and iron ore deposits, evolved to meet the need for armaments by Europe's swollen armies. This process of industrialization, accompanied by greater prosperity, in Bohemia and Moravia was to continue during the rest of the 19th century (whereas the mountainous region, Slovakia, remained agricultural).

Pan-Germanism and Pan-Slavism
Nationalism began as a German Romantic movement, for, unlike the French for example, the Germans were divided into many states until Prussia under Bismarck achieved unification in 1871. It amounted to a feeling that, just as individuals should be free to express and develop their personalities, so nations, based on ethnic affinity and language, should

be in a position to develop as politically free states. In the philosophy of J. G. Herder, the great apostle of nationalism, the world could be seen as a great family of nations. Among them was the Slav group of nations: including Russians, Poles, Serbo-Croats and Slovenes (eventually the Yugoslavs), Czechs and Slovaks (eventually Czechslovakia) and so on. German nationalism was soon further developed into the Pan-German (All-German) movement, which envisaged a situation whereby all Germans, effectively all German-speakers, from the Baltic to Bohemia, would be united in one 'Greater Germany'. And almost as a mirror image of this vision, many Slavs began to think in terms of some vast Pan-Slav confederation.

Jan Kollar, a Slovak enthusiast for Herder's ideas, wrote his epic, *Slava's Daughter* (1824), in this idealistic vein. His epic was not promoting any concrete political programme, rather it was an affirmation of a common Slav spirit and an assertion of 'roots' that paralleled the contemporary German national revival. *Slava's Daughter* was accompanied by a deluge of similarly patriotic works, as linguistic affinities between Slav languages were explored and codified, medieval literature was unearthed, and collections of folk songs and proverbs poured from the printing presses. All this literary and cultural enterprise was to be of immense long-term significance, because it meant, for example, that Czech, which was regarded as merely a workaday language for peasants and artisans (unlike German, the language of high culture), now began to acquire a higher status.

Religious differences
But even the most romantic Pan-Slavist could not get over certain uncomfortable realities, namely the great differences between the Slav peoples. For a start, there were potent religious divisions. Thus the Poles were devout Catholics but the Russians, and many of the Balkan Slavs under Turkish rule, were Orthodox Christians, and the Czechs, though having a strong Catholic tradition, also took pride in the ethical spirit of the early Protestant reform movement led by the Bohemian Jan Huss (1369–1415). And though some visionaries liked to wax lyrical about the rugged and wholesome qualities of Slav culture, as opposed to the played-out degeneracy of Western Europe, there was no getting away from the fact that tsarist 'Mother Russia' was as backward as it was reactionary, hardly an inspiration to those Slavs who combined their nationalist aspirations with hopes of democracy.

Empress Maria Theresa (above) and her son Joseph ruled their vast Hapsburg empire with a rod of iron, but they were enlightened leaders and instigated many reforms.

Although anxious to find their own national identity, the Austrian Slavs were far better off than their Balkan brothers. As part of the powerful Austro-Hungarian empire, Czech industry in Bohemia and Moravia – the Czech homeland – boomed (below) and was well able to support rural Slovakia (left).

The Czech dilemma

Wedged in as they were between Germans and Russians, pragmatic Czechs and Slovaks were inclined to think that their best bet lay with reform *within* the Austro-Hungarian Empire. At least they were ethnically strong within it (Slav peoples were a majority in fact), and, with greater prosperity and cultural self-confidence, their common efforts could perhaps lead to concessions from the imperial authorities in Vienna. One of the greatest exponents of this approach was Francis Palacky (1798—1876), the great Czech historian and 'father of the nation', who once went so far as to say: 'If there were no Austrian empire, we would have to create one.'

Palacky's greatest work, *The History of the Czech Nation in Bohemia and Moravia,* was another milestone in the Czech rediscovery of a national identity (though, as a typical paradox, the first volume, which appeared in 1836, was published in German, the language of academia and high culture). Though inspired by patriotic hopes, Palacky was above all a scholar and he repudiated unrealistic politics, especially any inclination to be romantic about Russia's potential as the patron of Slav national destinies. In this attitude he was joined by the extremely influential pamphleteer and journalist,

26

Mary Evans Picture Library

The German critic and poet Johann Herder was seen as an apostle of nationalism. He envisaged the world as a family of nations, free to develop as individuals but united by ethnic traditions and language. His work, which reflected his love of the simple life, and the folk lore and songs of country people (right) greatly influenced Slav nationalist writers.

Karel Havliček, who had actually worked in Russia as a private tutor and who was more inclined to look to Western Europe, as opposed to Russia for models for the Slavs' national struggles.

Leaders like Palacky and Havliček envisioned a thoroughly revamped Hapsburg empire, based on the Danube Valley but organized on a federal principle with autonomous units composed of Germans, Czecho-Slovaks, Polish-Ukrainians (in Galicia), Magyars, Serbo-Croats and Slovenes, Italians (in Lombardy) and Rumanians. Such a confederation in Central Europe would, they argued, be a safeguard against any aggressive moves by Germany and Russia, and, moreover, would inspire the world with proof that different nations could coexist in harmony within the boundaries of one great state. Unfortunately, neither the Austrian Germans nor the Hungarian Magyars were interested in turning the old empire into such a league of nations.

The year of revolutions

During that agitated year, 1848–9, the very existence of the Austro-Hungarian Empire seemed threatened by the revolts that flared up in Vienna, Budapest and Prague. But the Czechs and Slovaks remained on the whole loyal to the Hapsburgs and to the newly proclaimed 18-year-old emperor, Franz Joseph (r. 1848–1916). A Pan-German parliament assembled in Frankfurt and, along with Austrian Germans, the Austrian Slavs were invited to attend. But the Slavs demonstrated their suspicions of the German intentions by refusing to go and instead organized their own Pan-Slav Congress in Prague, presided over by Palacky.

Even before the unification of Germany under Bismarck's Prussia got underway – a militaristic process that more than confirmed original Slav

anxieties – the Czechs and Slovaks knew well that because German ambitions entailed the dissolution of the Austro-Hungarian Empire, they had nothing to gain from the Pan-German movement. A 'Greater Germany' would swallow up Slav aspirations for freedom by reducing them to a small minority. 'If there exist in Vienna people who ask to have your Frankfurt for their capital,' Palacky warned the Frankfurt assembly, 'we can only cry: Lord forgive them for they know not what they ask.'

But despite this general loyalty to Vienna, the Slavs (and indeed all other Hapsburg subjects) had many reservations about the regime they lived under, and the Pan-Slav Congress was interrupted by violence, after a demonstration by students and workers for democratic rights was attacked by the imperial militia. The radical Slav delegates immediately took up the barricades in an uprising that lasted for six days. Unlike the equivalent Hungarian revolt, the rebellion in Prague was easily crushed, however, because the Czechs were not wholeheartedly against Austria-Hungary in itself.

When the revolts in Vienna, Prague and Budapest had been put down, after a brief experiment with liberal democracy, Austria-Hungary reverted to

Jan Kollar (far right), like many Slavs at the time, dreamt of a great Pan-Slav confederation. His epic Slava's Daughter (right) helped put the Czech language on the literary map.

SLÁWY DCERA.

Lyřicko-epická básen

w pěti

Z P Ě W J C H

od

Jana Kollára.

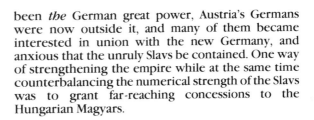

Úpelné wydánj.

absolute autocracy. For the next ten years Austria-Hungary was to be a 'prison of nations' and a new administrative constitution of 1860 put the Czechs at a further disadvantage because it gave voting rights to provincial assemblies only to taxpayers above a high income limit, thus enhancing the artificial supremacy of the German minority in Bohemia and Moravia.

Frustrated, Czech political leaders decided on a policy of non-cooperation and passive resistance towards the imperial authorities, boycotting sessions of the Imperial Council in Vienna. But strains within the Czech national movement now led to a new division between the 'Old Czechs', exemplified by Palacky, and the 'Young Czechs', who were beginning to look more to Russia. But even among the cautious old guard there was a new mood of defiance, especially after Austria-Hungary's defeat by Prussia in 1866 and the establishment of the new German Reich (after the defeat of France) in 1871: 'We existed before Austria and will survive her,' declared Palacky.

The formation of Bismarck's Germany had a very unsettling effect on the state of play between the nations within the Hapsburg empire. From having been *the* German great power, Austria's Germans were now outside it, and many of them became interested in union with the new Germany, and anxious that the unruly Slavs be contained. One way of strengthening the empire while at the same time counterbalancing the numerical strength of the Slavs was to grant far-reaching concessions to the Hungarian Magyars.

The Dual Monarchy

Accordingly, by the Dual Monarchy settlement of 1867 the Hapsburg empire was divided into two co-equal parts – Austria and Hungary – sharing their foreign policy and armed forces and united in the person of the monarch, Franz Joseph, who was now Emperor of Austria and King of Hungary. By this new arrangement the Czechs in Bohemia and Moravia remained within the Austrian part of the newly styled empire, but the Slovaks, with whom they had a close ethnic affinity and shared political aspirations, were left to the mercy of the Hungarians, whose own national aspirations took little account of such minorities.

In their struggle to be recognized as at least the equals of the Magyars, the Czechs had one new card to play – the immense strategic significance of Bohemia vis á vis the potentially threatening German Reich. Besides, they weren't even asking for complete home rule like the Hungarians, just more scope for their existing institutions and civil service. So the imperial authorities were persuaded to grant 18 'fundamental articles' to the Czechs in 1871, and the emperor signed a special edict promising to undergo coronation as king of Czechoslovakia to symbolize the new position of the old Czech crown lands (Bohemia, Moravia and part of Silesia) within his domain. But the Hungarians and the Austrian Germans were outraged and so when Bismarck reassured Vienna that the new Reich had no aggressive designs on Bohemia, the imperial authorities got cold feet and reneged on the commitments made to the Czechs.

Enter Mother Russia

For many Czechs and Slovaks the Dual Monarchy and the treachery over the 1871 'agreements' showed conclusively that there was no hope of a federated Central European state emerging from Austria-Hungary. Moreover, Germany's annexation of Alsace-Lorraine in 1871 held disturbing implications because its Germanness was largely based on the fact that the German language was spoken there. For Slavs disturbed by such portents Russia began to look more and more appealing, as indeed the only Slav great power had begun to look when Tsar Nicholas I had been succeeded by the more liberal Alexander II in 1855.

Many Russian intellectuals had visions of a great union of Slavs and since Russia's defeat in the Crimean War (1853–6) the government authorities looked more kindly on their ideas. In 1867 an 'ethnological exhibition', which was in fact the first Pan-Slav gathering to be held in Russia, was organized in Moscow. In order to welcome the 84 non-Russian Slav delegates from Austria-Hungary and the Balkans, the ladies of St Petersburg then opened their own branch of the 'Slavic Benevolent Association' and collected an imposing group of members, including not just intellectuals, but generals, ambassadors, judges and senior public officials. The arts were represented by none other than the great novelist Fyodor Dostoevsky and every honour, including a reception by the emperor and empress at the palace of Tsarsko Selo, was heaped upon the visitors. A sarcastic Austrian ambassador wrote:

With plans afoot to create a 'Greater Germany', the Austrian Slavs were keen to demonstrate their determination to retain their own identity. So they declined the invitation to attend the Pan-German assembly in Frankfurt and organized their own Pan-Slav Congress in Prague (above). The delegates of the Slavonic Congress in Prague, (left).

Germany's growing friendship with Turkey. And, in the long run, the sponsorship of foreign Slavs in time affected the development of the Russian revolutionary movement.

Economic and cultural consolations

Back in Austria-Hungary, many Czechs, particularly the urban middle-classes, were consoled by continuing economic advance, a boom in fact, which had been partly precipitated by the resented Dual Monarchy settlement. From 1878 the policy of passive resistance was abandoned by Czech politicians in favour of more active involvement in existing institutions. Although some sneered at them for pursuing a policy of 'breadcrumbs', Czech delegations to the Imperial Council and regional bodies did obtain some significant concessions, especially in relation to the official status of their

These gentlemen are for the moment the lions of St Petersburg. They are being dragged from one feast to another, and in the streets the people run after their carriages in order to see 'the Slavs'. One would suppose they had never seen any before, as though one had just discovered a new archipeligo (sic) in Polynesia . . .

But despite the rhetoric, there was an undeniable overlap between Russian imperialism and Russian-sponsored Pan-Slavism, and whereas this was more justifiable in the case of the Orthodox Slavs in the Balkans, many of whom did look to Russia as their religious protector during their struggles against Turkish oppression, it was hardly palatable to non-Orthodox Slavs. So the Congress in 1867 was not without its awkward aspects, notably the conspicuous absence of the Poles, who were unmoved by references to Slav brotherliness after the rebellion and shocking reprisals of 1863. (In fact the Poles often liked to think of their particular bit of Slavdom as 'Poland crucified between two thieves – Germany and Austria'.) So, notwithstanding the genuine goodwill and the festivities, nothing concrete came out of the 1867 Russian Pan-Slav Congress. The Slav visitors could not agree on a common literary language, there was no serious talk of mass conversions to the Orthodox church, and political federation was not even discussed. The whole jamboree had more significance within Russia, where Pan-Slavism was now endorsed by a government that was to be increasingly worried by

In a fit of rebellion, delegates from the Pan-Slav Congress joined students and workers at the barricades in an uprising that lasted six days (below).

Sub umbra alarum tuarum.

language. But even these useful reforms were still no answer to the lack of political direction in the face of the question: how were the Czech and Slovak peoples to pursue their national destiny in a state run basically by two minorities – Magyars and Germans – which was dominated on the one side by Germany and on the other by Russia?

As a compensation for the political dilemma, music, painting and sculpture, and literature flourished, the particular popularity of satire showing how important it was to find devious ways of dealing with thorny political realities. Because of its direct link with rural traditions and folk song, music was particularly important as a unifying and morale-raising force. Under the spell of music by Smetana (d. 1884), Dvořák (and, a little later, Janáček), the differences between townspeople and peasants, Catholics, Protestants and Jews, soldiers and students, Czechs and Slovaks, could be melted by an awareness of a shared cultural heritage.

This confidence and prosperity was reflected in the opening in 1881 of the National Theatre in Prague – with an opera by Smetana as its first performance – a new cultural venue to rival the old Theatre of the Estates, the primarily aristocratic venue where Mozart's *Don Giovanni* had had its first performance in 1787. Then, in 1882, Prague's Charles-Ferdinand University was divided into

To Czechs the Dual Monarchy of Austria-Hungary, symbolized by the two-headed eagle (far left), was as an oppressor and a threat to the creation of a federated central European State.

The assassination of Archduke Ferdinand – Franz Joseph's heir – at Sarajevo (left). Sarajevo in the Serbian province of Bosnia-Hercegovina, had become a centre for Slav nationalism and the incident was the event which sparked off World War 1.

In 1918 the Republic of Czechoslovakia was created, with its own national anthem and with Thomas Masaryk (right) as its president.

separate Czech and German institutions. And to take the chair of philosophy in the Czech university, Thomas G Masaryk (1850–1937) returned from Vienna University. At first this young academic was regarded as an impertinent outsider by local politicians, but Masaryk soon took on a prominent role in Prague politics.

The 'Realists'

Masaryk earned the adulation of his people because, like so many of his fellow Czechoslovaks, he started life as a poor boy, spoke plainly and lived simply. He received a higher education only after he had started to train as a blacksmith in a village in southern Moravia (near the Slovak border), and he received this education abroad, meeting his American wife when they were both studying in Leipzig in Germany. But his long absences abroad made him see problems more objectively and less romantically, and befitted him for a role as the Czechoslovak national conscience.

Masaryk followed on from the pragmatic traditions of Palacky and Havliček, making a characteristically sobering intervention in the so-called 'battle of the manuscripts', the controversy surrounding the Königinhofer forgery. In 1817 a passionately patriotic poet named Václav Handa had published 'ancient' Czech manuscripts detailing a great national saga, which he claimed to have 'discovered'. Naturally enough, this saga was greeted with great popular enthusiasm, for here was a drama that testified to the ancient lineage of the Slav national spirit and, later in the century, even rivalled the *Ring des Nibelungen,* which the Germans made such a fuss about. So even when the epic was proved to be a forgery, people were reluctant to accept the truth.

It was Masaryk who sternly declared that the Czechoslovak had no need of phony morale boosters and, as head of a new Realist Party, he urged a strategy of 'small jobs' (as opposed to vainglorious deeds). Like Palacky, Masaryk hoped for a federal solution to Austria-Hungary's multi-national ferment, and he was a great admirer of the American system. In his 'realism' and practical approach Masaryk was joined by another Czech political leader, Karel Kramar, who unlike him did see a role for Russia in the shaping of the Czechoslovak national destiny. However, Kramar, who was married to a Russian (just as Masaryk's wife was American) saw himself as a 'Neo-Slavist' as opposed to a Pan-Slavist. This meant that he was interested only in a cultural union of Slavs rather than a political union, and he in fact organized Prague's second Pan-Slav Conference in 1908, at which there were many Russian delegates. By encouraging good relations with Russia, Kramar hoped to bring Vienna and Moscow closer together, and drive Berlin and Vienna apart, but, as the stormclouds of the First World War gathered, such hopes were doomed.

The impact of the First World War

The First World War was directly precipitated by the national struggles of the Southern Slavs, for Austria-Hungary's annexation of the Serbian province of Bosnia-Hercegovina (now in Yugoslavia) was the provocation that resulted in the assassination of Archduke Ferdinand, Franz Joseph's heir, at Sarajevo. But it was obvious to many, as soon as the war broke out, that Austria-Hungary would not survive the struggle, and many Czechs and Slovaks saw no reason why they should support a dynasty that paid so little attention to their aspirations. Indeed, they naturally had more sympathy with the Allies (Russia, Serbia, France, Belgium and Britain) than with the Central Powers (Germany, Austria-Hungary and Turkey); small numbers of Slav soldiers in the Austro-Hungarian army surrendered to the Russians and then organized themselves into a legion in order to fight the Central Powers.

Even before the end of 1914 Masaryk went into voluntary exile to launch a campaign for an independent Czechoslovakia based on the assumption of an Allied victory, while Kramar's outspoken sympathy for Russia earned him imprisonment and a sentence of death. The time for 'small jobs' and 'breadcrumbs' was clearly passed.

When America entered the war on the Allied side in April 1917 – despite the disengagement of Bolshevik Russia from December 1917 – it looked as if the Central Powers could not win the war. Moreover, America's involvement was based on President Woodrow Wilson's '14 Points', which called for a peace settlement that would accommodate nationalist hopes for self-determination and set up a League of Nations. In keeping with Wilson's spirit, Masaryk's Czechoslovak National Committee in Paris was soon recognized by the Allies as the basis of a future government. Too late, did the new Hapsburg Emperor Charles (who succeeded Franz Joseph in 1916) reprieve Kramar from the death sentence and attempt to organize his inheritance into a federation of equal states organized along ethnic lines. By the peace treaty that ended the First World War the enormous Dual Monarchy of Austria-Hungary was no more – Austria itself was reduced to its German ethnic core, and forbidden to unite with Germany, and by 1920 Hungary had lost all of its non-Magyar territories to its neighbours.

Out of Bohemia, Moravia, part of Silesia and Slovakia, the Republic of Czechoslovakia was born in 1918, with Thomas Masaryk as its first president (until 1935). This revolution was very quiet. No blood was spilled and no force was used, though the porticos of various public buildings were slightly damaged by the removal of Hapsburg emblems. Remarkably, the fledgling state overcame the problems in amalgamating Masaryk's Paris-based National Committee with the Czechoslovak legionaries who had fought for the Allies and the National Committee that had been set up in Prague, and emerged as a democracy without undergoing the trauma of a civil war.

Townsfolk, peasants and the military join together to celebrate the birth of the independent and democratic state of Czechoslovakia. It was a happy time indeed – the revolution had been bloodless and the Austrian and Hungarian Slavs had won their long strugle for national identity.

THE GREAT COMPOSERS

Antonin Dvořák

1841–1904

Antonin Dvořák, the first internationally famous Bohemian composer, was greatly influenced by Slavic folk music. He did not copy folk songs note for note, however, but revealed his genius at transferring their spirit into the language of Romantic music. The finest of his compositions are deceptively simple and nostalgic, yet so enhanced by his gift of melody that their dramatic power is unmistakable. During a three-year stay in America, Dvořák became infatuated with native American music; his conflation of Bohemian melodies and American grass-roots music resulted in his Symphony no. 9, 'From the New World', analysed in the Listener's Guide. *With this work, he truly captured a musical expression of an emergent America, discussed in* In The Background. *His great musical imagination and open mind ensured the appeal of his compositions throughout the world.*

Antonin Dvořák's instinctive, melodic compositions gave him fame far beyond his Bohemian birthplace. As a child, he was sent from his small village to Prague to consolidate his musical gifts. He played in theatre orchestras during the 1860s; hard pressed for both time and money – even for the paper to compose upon – he still managed to write. He had begun to establish a following in Prague when, in 1875, a state grant from the Austrian government eased his financial worries and encouraged a burst of creative activity. His works attracted the attention of Brahms, who helped to bring his music to western Europe. His poignant work was soon in great demand, yet he remained a humble man, whose passions included railroads and birds. Successful visits to England and Moscow preceded a stay in America. His international reputation assured, he returned to Prague and composed until his death in 1904.

Archiv für Kunst und Geschichte

COMPOSER'S LIFE

'God-gifted composer'

At the height of his career, Antonín Dvořák was fêted from Moscow to the Mississippi. But he never forgot his Bohemian peasant childhood or the Czech people who inspired his music.

Antonin Dvořák was among the happiest of all composers. Unassuming, level-headed and natural, even at the height of his success, Dvořák – pronounced 'dVoorrshark' – suffered none of the mental anguish that seemed to afflict so many of the composers of the Romantic era, such as Tchaikovsky and Schumann. Throughout his life, despite many setbacks and reverses, Dvořák retained a simple, wholehearted delight in living, a delight that shines throughout his music and inspired deep affection in all who knew him.

In many ways, Dvořák is the spiritual heir of Schubert and their music has 'the same spontaneous and irrepressible flow of melody, the same delicate sense of instrumental colouring and the same instinctive command of the means of expression.' These words were actually used by Dvořák to describe Schubert, his favourite composer; but they apply equally well to himself.

Although during his lifetime he was fêted in London, Paris and New York, Antonin Dvořák remained at heart a country-loving man. The uncomplicated beauty of the Bohemian countryside (below and centre) was always a delight to him. It always gave him great pleasure to wander through the woodlands near his home at Vysoká – south of Prague, where from 1888 he spent his summers relaxing.

Dvořák's music is, like Schubert's, instantly approachable, and it was always his belief that music should above all entertain, not instruct. Indeed, few composers have had at their command such a rich fund of wonderful, memorable tunes, tunes that have become familiar throughout the world. Pieces like the *New World Symphony* and the *Slavonic Dances* flew straight to the hearts of the public and have remained there ever since.

Although fairly tall, about five foot eleven, Dvořák had the solid, stocky build of all Bohemian peasants, and the same broad, squat features. When he was younger, wild dark hair and a thick, bushy beard combined with a piercing gaze to give an effect so strikingly outlandish that the famous German conductor Hans von Bülow declared that Dvořák reminded him of Caliban, the monstrous character from Shakespeare's play *The Tempest*. Von Bülow also described Dvořák as 'next to Brahms, the most God-gifted composer of the present day'.

Pictures of the composer also give an impression of what one critic called grim 'bulldog ferocity' and it is easy to get an impression of Dvořák as a wild, irascible Bohemian. Nothing could be further from the truth.

Dvořák was born in 1841 in the small village of Nelahozeves (right), north of Prague. Despite the fact that his musical talent was abundantly obvious, his father František Dvořák (far right) intended that he should follow in his footsteps and become a butcher. However, after completing his apprenticeship one of his uncles, Antonín Zdeněk, offered to finance his full-time musical studies in Prague. On his arrival there he stayed with several relatives, amongst whom was his father's sister, Josefina Dušková (far right).

middle-aged, Dvořák would stroll down to the Franz Josef station in Prague early every day just to see the trains and take down their numbers. Nothing would please him more than to make friends with an engine driver. If he was teaching, he would send one of his pupils to discover which engine was hauling the Vienna express that day.

Dvořák had many other passions apart from trains. He was fascinated by birds, for instance, and the theme for the third movement of the *String Quartet in F* is inspired by the song of the scarlet tanager. When he bought his country home in Vysoká, he was able to indulge a long-cherished dream and breed pigeons. But his greatest passion was, of course, music and his enthusiasm for the art never once dimmed.

The Village Inn

Dvořák's passion for music started young. He was

Dvořák could indeed be tenacious and extremely obstinate. He seems to have had quite a temper – and on big public occasions he smiled but rarely. But all Dvořák's friends testify ardently to the real sweetness and gentleness of his nature, and loved him deeply for it. They loved him too for the simple pleasure he took in life, and the great joy he found in telling people about these pleasures. Any slowness to smile was simply natural modesty and humility. When his stern face wrinkled in laughter or he launched enthusiastically into one of his pet subjects, oblivious to the world, few could resist his warmth and humour. Tchaikovsky, who befriended Dvořák in 1888, referred to him as *'simpatichniy chudak'* – the dear funny fellow – and the normally testy Brahms seems to have had an even deeper affection for him – an affection that lasted a lifetime.

For Dvořák, life was a wonderful, happy thing and he looked on the great inventions of man with the wide-eyed delight of a child. When he was nine, a railway was built through his native village of Nelahozeves, only 25 years after the opening in England of the Stockton-Darlington railway. The young country boy was spell-bound and ever after had a tremendous fascination for trains. Even when

born, on 8th September 1841, in a low-ceilinged room above the inn in the village of Nelahozeves on the River Vltava. His father, František Dvořák, like František's father before him, was the inn keeper and butcher for the sleepy village – the two trades often went hand-in-hand in this part of the world. His mother Anna was the daughter of the bailiff at the local castle. Both young Antonín's grandfathers had been simple peasants, working the land, but by enterprise and sheer hard work, they had improved their status a little.

František Dvořák was an attractive and solidly-built man, accomplished not only in dispensing fine ale and meat but also, like so many of his fellow country-men, a capable musician.

Music was in the blood of all Czechs and they burst into song and dance at every occasion. Dvořák once said of the English that they did not love music; they merely respected it. The Czechs certainly loved it.

There always seemed something to celebrate in Nelahozeves. Like so many Bohemian villages, it seemed filled with an air of gaiety and optimism even when the weight of the Austrian Empire was at its heaviest.

It was not long before little 'Toník' too was caught

Dvořák's father was eventually persuaded to let Antonín follow a musical career and in September 1857 Dvořák set out for Prague (far right) to begin his studies at the Prague Organ School. When he graduated in 1859 he was awarded the second prize and told that 'his work was excellent but his musical theory was less sound than his practical work'.

When Dvořák was 13 he was sent to Zlonice the village where his Uncle Antonín lived, to continue his apprenticeship and to improve his grasp of German – then the official language. The German master at the Zlonice school (right) was also the church organist and under his guidance Dvořák learned piano, organ, viola, violin and keyboard harmony.

by this exuberant musical spirit, and it seems that he was playing simple dance tunes on the fiddle for the benefit of customers in the inn before he was five years old. Before long, helped by the local schoolmaster and organist Josef Spic, Tonik was playing alongside his father in the band at weddings and other local festivals.

Music soon became everything to the little boy. But when he was 11 years old and his time at the local village school came to an end, Tonik was naturally apprenticed to his father in the butcher's trade. He took badly to the trade and dreaded going to fetch a heifer from the next village – the heifer invariably dragged him through the mud.

In the days of Austrian domination, it was essential to speak German if you wanted to get on in any trade. So after a year of apprenticeship at butchering, Tonik was sent to stay in the small town of Zlonice, 15 miles away, with his uncle Antonín Zdeněk (Anna's

brother). There, his parents hoped he would learn German from a teacher at the local school, Antonín Liehmann.

From Zlonice to Prague

Liehmann had a fiery temper and was a strict disciplinarian, but he was also a dedicated and highly competent musician. He was so delighted by his new pupil's rapid progress on organ, viola and piano, that he began to teach Tonik harmony and counterpoint and invited him to join his small orchestra – the German studies were inevitably neglected.

Soon Toník may have tried his hand at composition. He was so proud of his first polka, so the story goes, that he took it back to Nelahozeves for the local band to play. Unfortunately, he had not realized that the cornet is a transposing instrument and music must be written in a different key from that in which it is to be played. Poor Tonik's composing debut was slightly less harmonious than he anticipated.

After a year Tonik's parents joined him when František took over The Big Inn in Zlonice. Toník's musical activities were curtailed a little, and, in 1856, he may have actually completed his apprenticeship as a butcher. A year in the Silesian village of Česká Kamenice improved his German (and his music) no end. But his father desperately needed his help in the inn, which was in difficulties because of the landlord's vindictive attitude towards a 'foreigner'.

Liehmann couldn't bear to see his star pupil's musical talent go to waste, so he persuaded Toník's Uncle Antonín Zdeněk to put up the money to send

PRAGUE

the boy to the Organ School in Prague. Liehmann's pleadings were successful and, in late September 1857, Tonik, then 16 years old, set out with his father and a hand cart piled with his belongings to walk the 26 miles south to the great city of Prague – they could not afford a train ticket.

The young musician was never really at ease in the imposing surroundings of the Organ School, partly because only those who spoke German well seemed to get favourable treatment. He acquired a rudimentary knowledge of the old classical masters, Mozart and Beethoven, but never seriously threw himself into the study of musical theory. At the end of his time at the school, his teachers described him as 'excellent, but inclined to show a more practical talent. Practical knowledge and accomplishment appear to be his aim; in Theory he achieves less.'

It was playing the viola in the St Cecilia Society Orchestra that he really enjoyed. The leader of this orchestra, Antonín Apt, was an ardent admirer of Richard Wagner, a composer whose work was frowned upon by the rather staid Organ School. Soon the impressionable young viola player was equally enthusiastic about Wagner's heady, intoxicating music. For Dvořák, the spell of Wagner's music was to last many years – he even wrote an opera, *Alfred,* in Wagnerian style about the Anglo-Saxon king Alfred the Great.

Dvořák married Anna Cermáková (right), one of his former pupils and the sister of his first love Josefina, in 1873.

The young musician

When Dvořák finished at the Organ School in 1860, his family was still desperately poor and unable to support him. Fortunately, a Prague band-leader Karel Komzák was in need of a viola player and Dvořák willingly accepted the job. The band was very popular in restaurants in Prague and was often asked to play at balls and classical concerts.

Meanwhile, as a sop to nationalist feelings the Habsburgs began to grant a few minor concessions to their subject nations. For the Czechs, this included the founding of a Czech National Theatre to stage Czech plays and operas and foreign operas in Czech translations. The Czech nationalist composer Bedřich Smetana (see pages 7-15) was to play a key role in the theatre, and many of his operas, such as *The Bartered Bride* received their premières there.

Komzák's band was to form the nucleus of the orchestra at the theatre and so Dvořák actually played at many of these premières. During his nine years in the theatre orchestra, from 1862 to 1871, Dvořák played in a wide range of new and interesting works such as Gounod's *Faust* and Glinka's *Ruslan and Lyudmila* and more than made up in practical experience what he had failed to learn in theory at the Organ School. More importantly he was exposed to the works of Czech nationalist composers and shown just what potential there was in his own national heritage.

In his spare time, Dvořák composed and gave lessons to supplement his income. He told no one but his closest friends about his compositions, which included his first couple of symphonies. Although none of these early works receive much attention now, in their composition Dvořák was slowly but surely coming to grips with his craft. Yet after 12 years, there was still little to suggest he would be anything more than a minor composer.

During this time, one of Dvořák's music pupils was Josefina Cermáková, the pretty 16-year old daughter of a Prague goldsmith. Antonín fell deeply in love with her and wrote a song cycle, *Cypresses,* in her honour. Sadly, his ardour was not reciprocated. But as he continued to teach in the Cermák household over the years, his eye eventually fell upon her younger sister Anna. Anna had a fine contralto voice and at the age of 16, began to sing in the chorus at the Provisional Theatre. Clearly there were plenty of occasions for the young couple to get together, and by the time Anna's father's objections to their marriage were removed (by his death in 1872), Anna was already pregnant.

Anna and Antonín were married on 17 November 1873, and their marriage was long and happy. Indeed, Dvořák's marriage coincided with a slow but steady upturn in the quality of his music and his fortunes as a composer. In 1874, he received his first major première, with Smetana conducting the overture to *King and Charcoal Burner* (a drastically revised version of the sub-Wagnerian opera *Alfred).* A year later, he was fortunate enough to win the Austrian State Stipendium offered to poor young artists in the Western half of the Empire.

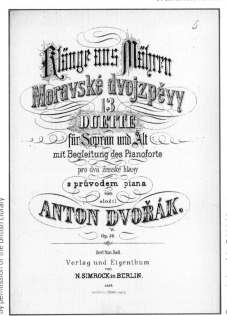

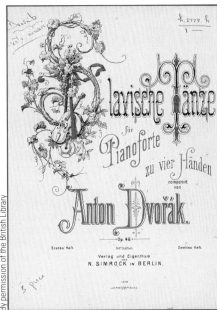

Dvořák's first invitation to conduct his own work abroad came from the Philharmonic Society in London. At the first of three public performances in March 1884 he conducted Stabat Mater at the Royal Albert Hall (below).

Encouraged by this success, Dvořák was spurred to a burst of creative activity and in four months a stream of beautiful music flowed from his pen, including various pieces of chamber music, the lovely *Serenade for Strings,* the *Moravian Duets* and his first symphony of real merit, No 5 in F Major.

The following year, Dvořák entered, and won, the Stipendium again and was freed from his main financial worries. But his music was still heard only by a small circle of Czech musicians. By chance, one of the panel judging the Stipendium was the composer Johannes Brahms. When Dvořák entered for the award for the fourth time in 1878, Brahms wrote to his publisher Simrock, recommending the *Moravian Duets.*

When you play them through you will be as pleased as I am, and, as a publisher, taken by their piquancy . . .Dvořák has written all kinds of music . . .and is very talented. He is also very poor! I beg you to think the matter over!

Simrock published the *Duets* widely and they were an instant success. He followed these up with Dvořák's *Slavonic Dances.* Western Europeans were charmed by the fresh, lyrical sound and exciting rhythms of this very Bohemian (to western ears) music and Dvořák was soon in terrific demand.

At that time, however, three events clouded his life, the deaths of his three children in quick succession, – Josefa two days after her birth in 1876, 11 month old Ružena by swallowing phosphorous, when accidentally left unsupervised in August 1877, and Otakar just three weeks later from smallpox. In his grief, Dvořák returned to and completed the *Stabat Mater,* a religious choral work first started three years earlier. It was this lovely and poignant work, more than anything, which was to consolidate his success abroad.

It was the *Stabat Mater* which was performed in the Albert Hall on 20 March 1884, giving Dvořák one of his greatest public triumphs.

As soon as I appeared, I received a tempestuous

welcome from the audience of 12,000. These ovations increasing, I had to bow my thanks again and again, the orchestra and choir applauding with no less fervour. I am convinced that England offers me a new and certainly happier future, one which I hope may benefit the Czech art.

Dvořák was right. The English had indeed taken him into their hearts. A round of banquets and receptions ensued and newspapers carried lengthy articles on him and Czech music. His popularity in England was assured and in all he made nine happy trips to England over the next 15 years.

After his great success in England Dvořák was at last financially secure and he celebrated by realizing a long-cherished dream – he bought a small house in the country where he and his family could spend the summer. The house was at Vysoká on land belonging to Count Kaunitz (who had married Dvořák's first love Josefa) and Dvořák's life here proved to be

In 1892 Mrs Jeanette Thurber (above left), founder of the National Conservatory in New York, invited Dvořák to be its Director. In all, Dvořák spent three years in America, mainly in New York, (above) where amongst other things he enjoyed riding on the 'El' – the over-head tram system! Very homesick, he arranged to spend his summer holidays in the Czech community of Spillville, Iowa. In the summer of 1893 he stayed in the house (below) on Main Street, Spillville.

From Spillville Dvořák made an excursion to the Chicago World Fair (left) to attend the celebrations for Czech Day on 12 August 1893. He conducted a programme of his works including three Slavonic Dances *and the Eighth Symphony, and attended a banquet in his honour organized by the Chicago Circle of Czech Musicians.*

WILLS'S CIGARETTES

DVORÀK

Although the source of his inspiration was firmly rooted in the Bohemian countryside and people, Dvořák's international reputation established him as a celebrity far beyond its borders. Indeed, such was his popularity that he was, posthumously, included as a subject in a cigarette card series of Musical Celebrities issued in 1912 (above).

blissfully happy. Early every morning while at Vysoka, he went for long rambles through the woodlands. During the day, he composed in the summer house or pottered in the garden. In the evening, he went down to the village inn to drink, sing and tell stories with the peasants and miners.

Over the next nine years, his success was consolidated and he was showered with an increasing number of awards and honours, including the Austrian 'Iron Crown' and a Doctorate of Music at Cambridge, England. He continued to compose and wrote many masterpieces, great and small. His life was spent working in Prague – teaching at the Conservatory, composing or conversing in coffee bars; relaxing at home in Vysoká with the family; or performing on one of his many trips abroad. But in 1891, he received a telegram that was to change this routine.

WOULD YOU ACCEPT DIRECTOR NATIONAL CONSERVATORY OF MUSIC NEW YORK OCTOBER 1892 ALSO LEAD SIX CONCERTS OF YOUR WORKS

At first, he took little notice of this unusual telegram, but the sender persisted. The sender was Mrs Jeanette Thurber, the wife of a millionaire New York grocer, who had founded the American Opera Company and the National Conservatory of Music. Her aim in founding the Conservatory was to establish a national American school of composition, and Dvořák, the leading nationalist composer, seemed the ideal person to set the ball rolling. Dvořák was taken with the idea, particularly when he found that the Conservatory was open to all, regardless of means

and colour. He was also taken by the salary, a princely $15,000. So, in September 1892, he set sail for New York.

Dvořák's time in America was immensely successful, and he found many new friends and fans and wrote much music, including the famous symphony *From the New World.* But he was never really happy there, away from his family and beloved country. So when Mrs Thurber ran into financial difficulties during his second period in New York and was unable to pay him, he was relieved to find an excuse to go home once again.

Among the many beautiful works that Dvořák wrote in the last eight years of his life are the operas *The Devil and Kate, Armida* and *Rusalka.* In these works, Dvořák finally realized his ambition to write a genuine Czech opera to match the masterpieces of Smetana. Both *The Devil and Kate* and *Armida* were relatively successful, but it was the beautiful, atmospheric *Rusalka,* based on a libretto by the Czech poet Kvapil, which was the real triumph. Rarely performed abroad, it is regarded with deep affection by Dvořák's fellow countrymen and holds a place of high honour in the national heritage. It was a fitting summation to a rich life's work.

Dvořák died suddenly on May Day 1904. After a month's illness, he had finally been given permission by the doctor to get up and join the May Day celebrations. But after the meal, he suddenly felt dizzy, and slumped in his chair unable to speak. He was carried to his room while the doctor was called, but moments later he had died. Few composers can have been so greatly missed by their fellow countrymen.

Symphony no. 9 'From the New World'

By skilfully blending Bohemian melodies with the richly contrasting rhythms of American grass-roots music, Dvořák created his Symphony no. 9, a much loved masterpiece 'From the New World'.

Few composers have been more open-minded to the spell of external musical forces than Dvořák. He revered the great classical masters of the past – Haydn, Mozart, Beethoven – but was equally influenced by the music of his contemporaries and, for example, incorporated various Wagnerian ideas into his early symphonies (though not wholly successfully). The growing movement of Czech nationalism, as exemplified in the music of his compatriot Smetana, also affected him and helped to give his music a specific, Slavonic character.

Dvořák retained this open-mindedness all his life and, when he was invited to America at the age of 50, he made it his business to seek out the best elements of what was to him a new and exciting culture, one that was tinged with the deep melancholy of Black slave music and the exotic, other-worldly, chants of the American Indians.

As a competition judge, he noticed what he described to a friend as 'other ideas, other colourings', in the music of young white composers. Later he went so far as to say that the future of American music lay in

The 'New World' Symphony was the very first work Dvořák composed in America, and the freshness and energy of the music seems to capture the composer's initial excitement at stepping out on the bustling streets of New York (left).

its 'native' culture. It is evident that he attempted to show America the way by writing what was considered to be the first truly American symphony; yet he repeatedly denied that he had done anything more than compose 'in the spirit' of native American music. He certainly caught the brashness of city life there and, even though he never travelled far from the East Coast, the first conductor of his symphony (Anton Seidl) considered that the slow movement depicted the desolation of the far Western prairies to perfection.

Dvořák had read a Czech translation of Longfellow's epic poem, *Hiawatha* before going to America and was, therefore, already partly acquainted with aspects of American Indian culture (albeit at one remove and in a romantically 'artistic' form!), but apparently he had little opportunity to study their native music until after he had already completed his New World Symphony.

Black music, however, was another matter. In his capacity as head of the National Conservatory of Music in New York he came to know the black singer Harry Burleigh and was fascinated by the negro spirituals he sang. Dvořák would study them closely on paper, then invite Burleigh to sing them over, stopping him ever and again as some unexpected melodic twist or rhythmic felicity took his ear. 'Is that *really* the way you people sing?' he would enquire intently. Burleigh, an intelligent and patient student, ensured that the great composer transcribed his songs accurately and would point out where the sheet music of the spirituals differed in detail from the melodies he had carried in his head all his life.

But Dvořák had the true composer's gift of an inexhaustible musical imagination. In employing Czech folk music in his concert pieces he never merely copied. He studied its rhythms and melodic shape, transforming it into a higher art form while at the same time capturing its unmistakable essence. So it was, too, with Harry Burleigh's music. Tracing the course of the symphony, there are several instances where Dvořák almost certainly took elements of Black music as his basic material, but most are sublimated so skilfully into the tapestry of the music that the symphony never degenerates into anything like a scrapbook of American folk tunes.

For most of his three years in America (1892-95), Dvořák stayed in New York. He delighted in its hustle and bustle, its breathless energy and its noise. As an ardent train enthusiast, he loved the railways there, and a journey on New York's elevated line ('The El') particularly thrilled him. Whenever his duties at the Conservatory permitted, he seized the chance to get out into the busy streets and absorb their excitement along with their dust and din. And if, during these excursions, he was ever tempted to investigate the 'dives' which New York

The Ninth Symphony was one of five symphonies published by Simrock during Dvořák's lifetime. They were numbered according to their order of publication: thus the 'New World' Symphony was formerly known as 'No. 5' (above).

spawned in such profusion, he would have met yet another bright new musical experience: 'ragtime'.

The first piano rag to be published came out in 1897, but public interest in the form had been strong long before then. Ragtime sets a strenuously syncopated melody (in the right hand) against a steady, march-like rhythm (in the left), so that the 'time' is constantly displaced rhythmically and appears to be 'sprung forward'. The word 'rag' is probably short for 'ragged', which describes the effect admirably. Ragtime's catchy rhythms were a craze in American cities in the 1890's: it was an 'underground' music that was soon to bubble to the surface and take the world by storm.

From his arrival in New York at the end of September 1892, until shortly before Christmas that year, Dvořák was deeply involved in musical activities, adjudications, concert-giving, teaching and completing a cantata in honour of his host country – *The American Flag*. Then, on 20th December, he started work on the Symphony, scribbling down melodies based on the impressions he had absorbed. Once they had crystallized in his mind, he worked quickly, moulding them into a closely organized symphonic form. The first three movements were completed in sketch form by the end of January 1893 and were fully scored by 10th April. Only then did he start on the last movement – and this, too, was completed by 24th May. The creation of one of the most popular works in the entire repertoire, from first jottings to final score, had taken just over five months.

At the end of the first performance – given in Carnegie Hall on 16 December – Dvořák was compelled 'to stand like a king' and receive the thunderous applause. He

For Dvořák, the influence of America, which he thought must be felt by anyone 'with a nose at all', lay in its rich native culture – in particular, its folk song and plantation music (left). 'The music of the people', he told Harper's magazine, 'is like a rare and lovely flower growing amidst encroaching weeds. Thousands pass it, while others trample it underfoot.' Black spirituals had a profound impact on him, and he invited one of his black students, Harry T. Burleigh, who had transcribed many plantation melodies, (right), to sing to him. Dvořák's attentiveness is revealed in his inspired use of black melodies in the 'New World' Symphony: indeed the English horn in the second movement echoes the quality of Burleigh's voice.

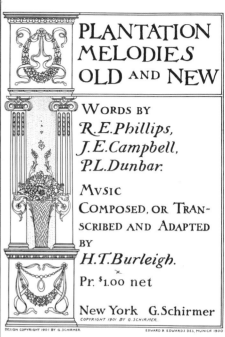

PLANTATION MELODIES OLD AND NEW

WORDS BY
R.E.Phillips,
J.E.Campbell,
P.L.Dunbar.

MVSIC COMPOSED, OR TRAN-SCRIBED AND ADAPTED BY
H.T.Burleigh.

Pr. $1.00 net

New York G.Schirmer

COPYRIGHT 1901 BY G.SCHIRMER.

DESIGN COPYRIGHT 1901 BY G.SCHIRMER.   EDWARD B EDWARDS DES, MUNICH 1900

later wrote, in obvious delight, 'the newspapers said that never before has a composer had such a triumph'.

A week later, the Symphony was played in Boston with such success that it had to be repeated the following week and, when Dvořák brought it home and conducted its first European performance at the National Theatre, Prague, he once again received rapturous applause. Since then it has never dropped out of the top ten of favourites and, for example, is performed at the Royal Festival Hall, London, more often than any other symphony.

Programme notes

'From the New World' is the last of Dvořák's nine symphonies. He himself called it 'No. 8', because he discounted his very first symphony, and generations following him went so far as to dismiss his first *four* symphonies. Therefore, for years, *From the New World* was called 'No. 5'. Today, all of Dvořák's symphonies are published and circulated, and this last work now bears the number 9.

First movement: Adagio-Allegro molto

Lower strings begin with a thoughtfully drooping melody and pause briefly as two horns give voice to a plaintive call. The woodwind take up this reflective mood but, before they can think too deeply they are rudely interrupted by a series of dramatic, syncopated 'ragtime' chords punctuated by timpani. Flutes and oboes then elaborate on the ragtime motif in two bright, colourful statements. Between these brisk passages, however, comes one of the most vital melodies in the whole symphony, powerfully syncopated, swelling and fading on horns, violas and cellos and eventually forming the main theme of this movement:

Example 1

2 horns *p* ———————— *f*
(with violas and cellos)

The thoughtfulness of the start is swept aside by strong gestures and decisive drumstrokes, and the Allegro molto enters confidently with the main theme on resounding horns. It is answered by a rhythmic figure on clarinets and bassoons

that gives a pulsating impetus both to this movement and, later, to the finale. But it is the main theme which dominates now, forcing the music into a pitch of high excitement. Then a brief interruption on violas and cellos provides a transition to the second theme. They quieten the music and, when the flutes and oboe take up the theme, they ring out clear and true above the strings.

The violins evidently approve of this newcomer, for they adopt it with alacrity, while the cellos strum a simple, banjo-like accompaniment. When the lowest strings begin to play, the tension mounts. The violins call out their challenge and the woodwind softly answers. Relentlessly, the composer now telescopes the old spiritual tune 'Swing low, sweet chariot' (placing it low on the flute and matching its opening rhythm to that of the main theme). At this point, all the musical ideas in the movement have been introduced and it is time to move on to the 'working-out' section, in which they are skilfully mixed into a complex symphonic statement.

'Swing low' is examined first. Horn and piccolo play the melody through; the trumpet swells on its second half, recalling the clarinet and bassoon idea of the main theme. The oboes immediately seize upon this fragment and, in no time at all, 'Swing low' and the main theme are standing side by side in equal importance. A long stretch of exciting development follows but, at its end, the main theme emerges triumphant. Championed by the woodwind, it is finally taken over and carried on a 'lap of honour' by the horns.

Apart from detail differences and the selection of new keys, this is the path of the development and the two themes can be heard chattering together as it unwinds.

Understanding music: music in America

Music in Europe had developed under two powerful institutions, the Church and the aristocracy. In America, music had to find a niche in the market place.

Sacred music arrived with the first religious settlers but the development of musical institutions was a slow process in colonial America. The first singing schools were established in New England in the 1720s and the publications of the first American composers, such as William Billings *New England Psalm Singer,* appeared in 1770.

Secular music in this period was still dependent on visiting European performers, but after America gained independence in 1776, and the cities along the Atlantic seaboard developed prosperous families with time for music, more European teachers and performers came to stay. By the end of the 19th century, Boston, New York and Philadelphia had symphony orchestras.

With the growth of a large middle class, musicians such as Lowell Mason (1792-1872) and George Root (1820-95) were able to influence music making in both, school and home. Mason introduced music in to the education system, and Root, his pupil, wrote and published popular Civil War songs.

But the real business of America was manufacture. Pianos made their way into the parlours of nearly every genteel American home and there was a great vogue for sentimental salon pieces. Even Louis Moreau Gottschalk (1829-69), a piano virtuoso with a talent in the order of Liszt and Thalberg, wrote a number of such pieces. However, Gottschalk himself was one of the few to make specifically American music, composing startling piano pieces with titles like *Bamboula* and *Le Bananier* based on Negro plantation melodies, which caused a sensation when he played them in Europe.

But it is Stephen Foster (1826-64) who came to be known as 'America's minstrel', who is best remembered today for his gentle, sentimental songs such as *Old Folks at Home, Jeannie with the light brown hair* and *Beautiful Dreamer;* and his 'Ethiopian' minstrel songs, such as *Camptown Races* and *Oh! Susannah.*

Later in the century, John Philip Sousa (1854-1932) and his band toured the world with a mixed repertory including his own stirring patriotic marches such as *The Stars and Stripes forever* which Sousa believed 'should make a man with a wooden leg step out.'

But for music at its highest level, the United States for long had to turn to Europe. Dvorak was by no means the only visitor. Tchaikovsky, Puccini, Sibelius and Richard Strauss were all drawn by lucrative offers. Not that America loved all these men brought with them. Elgar, on one of his several visits to the States, denied a request to lead a meeting to pray for the failure of Strauss's *Salome.* Great conductors – Mahler and Toscanini, for example, and pianists such as Rachmaninov and Horowitz were also tempted by the money that America could find to reward the artist. In the 1930s and 40s, the political events in Europe made the New World into a new home for Martinù, Bartók, Schoenberg and Stravinsky. Others, like Britten, Hindemith and Milhaud stayed for a period and then returned to Europe.

All this enriched music *in* America. But what of *American* music?

The father of modern American music was Charles Ives (1874-1954) – a successful businessman. Ives was trained by his father and at Yale, but he did not pursue a professional, musical career. His music is full of American resonances – old Stephen Foster tunes, barn dances, familiar hymns and Sousa marches. But these sounds were drawn together in such an innovative, startlingly original way – often with separate tunes played in differing keys and rhythms simultaneously – that they were not appreciated for decades.

Lacking a tradition, American composers in this century have done what the English and the central Europeans had done earlier, and turned to their own native music, the hymns of their founding fathers and the spirituals and jazz of their black compatriots.

Some of those elements are well illustrated in Copland's great ballet score of 1944, *Appalachian Spring,* with its country dance forms accompanying a revivalist meeting and its variations on the Shaker folksong, *The gift to be simple.* Indeed, the American ballet repertory contains such essentially American titles as Copland's *Rodeo* (1942) and *Billy the Kid* (1938) and Thomson's *Filling Station* (1937).

Today, the United States produces some of the finest musicians from world-renowned music schools such as the Curtis Institute in Philadelphia or the Julliard School in New York. Major symphony orchestras exist in all the main cities and continue to attract the best in world talent; while New York reigns undisputed as the dance capital of the world. Where once America lagged behind, it has now not only caught up, but threatens to overtake — unfettered by tradition but with a legacy of the pioneering spirit and well-endowed institutions, it is ideally suited for expanding music's frontiers.

The music of the black slaves on the plantations provided the inspiration for generations of American musicians from Foster to Copland.

But, when the coda (the final part) arrives to round off the movement, Dvořák builds it into a dramatic climax in which the main theme emphatically relives its moment of glory.

Second movement: Largo

It is often claimed that we owe the rich and colourful harmonies of the main subject of this movement – a solo cor anglais (English horn) supported by string harmonies and woodwind embellishments – to Dvořák's desire to capture the quality of Harry Burleigh's voice as he sang spirituals to the composer. That may be true. What is not true, however, is the equally widespread claim that this broad melody is a faithful representation of the spiritual 'Goin' Home'. Those nostalgic words were fitted to the tune much later – by one of Dvořák's pupils, William Fisher.

A sequence of stately chords commences the movement and these are repeated with modifications after the moving theme, Goin' Home, has been stated in full. Violins and cellos meditate on the melody (which must have touched the home-sick composer very deeply) before cor anglais, then two muted horns linger lovingly over fragments of it.

There is a change of mood and a slight increase in pace as flute and oboe announce a new theme with a prominent feature of three descending notes:

Example 2

Dvořák had, previously, sketched out scenes for a 'Hiawatha' opera that he never completed: it is probable that the sombre music he had written for Minnehaha's funeral found its way into this Largo as the elegiac central melody. This is easy to believe when one considers the restrained passion of the music and the grave beauty of the woodwind melody which follows, announced softly over a stalking, plucked bassline and against trembling interjections from the violins. As the music continues with great dignity, we may imagine the plaintive cries of mourners at an Indian funeral.

Suddenly, irreverently, a perky oboe melody enters and is whisked away by the flute. The sad mood is briefly broken as more and more instruments join together in a splendid, brassy blaze of music. Calm is quickly restored however. The cor anglais repeats its tune and is echoed haltingly by a small group of muted strings. After the nostalgic opening chords have softly sounded one more time, the movement comes gently to its close.

Third movement: Scherzo: Molto vivace

This movement had its origins in the Hiawatha opera once again, being representative of the jubilation during a wedding feast – though it has certainly

been radically enlarged and altered to make a full-scale symphonic movement whose bucolic energy perfectly balances the nobility of the preceding slow movement.

Impetuous chords, topped by the shrill jangle of triangle, evolve into a dancing rhythm over which the main subject is heard: a fragmentary, argumentative tune that loses its rhythmic way and has to be rounded up by loud drum interjections. When all the orchestra seem to agree at last, the music returns to the beginning to try again.

Violins and bassoon are left to repeat the last word of the disagreement, in preparation for what sounds like a plantation

work song – a sweet, soaring melody over a halting accompaniment. This is developed and enriched with great beauty of scoring and detail, the triangle adding its voice here, the rhythmic accompaniment becoming more jerky there, and then it is sung out, just once, in the rich tones of the cellos.

But the main subject soon bounces back, anxious to continue its argument. As a crescendo builds, there in the middle voices of the orchestra, we may catch a brief hint of resistance (the main theme from the first movement!) but this is swept away in the swirling climax.

That momentary dissent, however, is enough to disturb the music. Losing

ently the argumentative theme protests, this majestic, if now angry, horn theme prevails, only to be robbed of victory by an unexpected interloper. It is the first movement's 'Swing low' theme that has the last word.

Fourth movement: Allegro con fuoco
Reports of Dvořák's own handling of this last movement suggest that he took the opening bars very deliberately and then gradually increased their speed. This exaggerated style of conducting is no longer fashionable, but, if the listener can imagine it, it is possible to detect some connection between the building speed of the movement and the composer's well-documented love of railways, the first strokes seem so descriptive of a powerful locomotive gathering momentum. Once gathered, that momentum leads to an imperious new theme on horns and trumpets.:

Soon after arriving in the USA, Dvořák toyed with the idea of writing an opera based on Longfellow's Hiawatha *– a book he had enjoyed in Czech translation. The idea never really got off the ground, but two sketches found their way into the 'New World' Symphony: the death of Minnehaha, with its restrained mood of melancholy (left), became the famous central melody of the Largo, while Hiawatha's feast – a whirling, festive dance (below) – formed the basis of the Scherzo.*

A quick flourish on violins, and the theme is repeated even more incisively, to be stated yet again as all the strings urge the orchestra to action. Their prodding leads to a furious jig in which woodwind swirl smoothly around the somewhat detached notes of the strings. As the 'dancers' run out of steam, the jig degenerates into a jerky rhythm and only the clarinet can summon up the energy for a long, smooth theme. In majestic tones, the music grows louder, pouncing on fragments of the original rhythm and turning it into a kind of musical pun.

Then, unexpectedly, an odd three-note descending motif in woodwind – 'Three Blind Mice' – can be heard. The mice scuttle away leaving a solo bassoon muttering to itself in what may be an echo of a slaves' ditty. It is not alone for long, however; suddenly the 'Three Blind Mice' motif is shrilled out by the woodwind. Their call leads to two statements of the main subject on horns, the second hoisted up unexpectedly at its end. It alternates for a while with elements of the wild jig which again collapses to make way for the slow movement's melody (Goin' Home) on flutes and clarinet. The argumentative theme from the third movement returns and, while the flutes and clarinet build their melody into the main theme of this last movement, violas quietly play a running phrase redolent of the sad, solo bassoon's slave ditty.

Such a virtuoso marshalling of forces shows Dvořák's immense skill in unifying his symphony and makes clear why he needed to complete the first three movements before he could start work on the finale. The slow melody of the Largo is now spiced up as the music increases in

confidence, it fades away to be confronted by a stark and threatening statement on the cellos. Enough of frivolity, they seem to say, but the music disagrees: violins seize three of its scolding notes and run off with them tantalizingly as woodwind enter with a dancing, almost insolent melody that seems to take the dissenting fragment as a starting point and turn it into a garrulous caricature of itself. The dance continues in broad sunshine, strings and woodwind cooing alternately in carefree delight.

Eventually the first part of the movement is repeated in full and, just as it has run its course, the moment comes for the sombre mood to seek revenge – this time through the horns. No matter how vehem-

Glenbow Museum, Calgary

power and, reinforced by the argumentative theme, the two ideas become inseparable, totally dependent upon one another. But Dvořák is not yet ready to spring his biggest surprise: after brash, jagged chords the temperature falls and the music quietens. Violins and cellos recall the earlier clarinet melody leading the way into a broad and peaceful scene that shows the composer's ingenuity as a maker of glorious melody that never stays stationary – the swelling lower strings

always maintain the momentum of the music.

Soon the bassoon enters with its slaves' ditty and a solo horn introduces the main theme from the first movement . . .almost bursting with excitement at its rediscovery. The whole orchestra acclaims its arrival. It is greeted in turn by the horn theme of the finale and then the wild jig, as the music reaches an almost unbearable peak of excitement. Now comes the moment that Dvořák has so patiently

prepared: amid hammering timpani the stately chords which opened and closed the slow movement return with thrilling impact.

In the final moments of the symphony, most of its well-known characters pass before us, as if in a farewell parade. Then the work hurries to its close, with only the last, lingering chord reluctant to leave the stage.

It is impossible to say how much of the music was directly influenced by Dvořák's

Claude Monet 'La Gare Saint Lazare'. Reunion des musées nationaux

experiences in the US. Although the symphony was hailed as the first truly American creation, the Bohemian influence is strong and, overall, 'From the New World' is a Czech masterpiece. In the composer's own words, his symphony simply conveys 'impressions and greetings' of a new world but he also insisted many times:

'I never would have written it quite like that if I had never seen America'.

Dvořák's love of railways (left) seems to have left its mark on the fourth movement of the 'New World' Symphony. The music begins tentatively, gradually gathering steam and momentum, just like a powerful locomotive building up speed.

The public rehearsal of the symphony on 15 December 1893 was a sensational success. The **New York Herald** *carried a review the following day (right), describing how 'a large audience of usually tranquil Americans' were 'enthusiastic to the point of frenzy . . . and applauding like the most excitable 'Italianissimi' in the world'.*

DR. DVORAK'S GREAT SYMPHONY.

"From the New World" Heard for the First Time at the Philharmonic Rehearsal.

ABOUT THE SALIENT BEAUTIES.

First Movement the Most Tragic, Second the Most Beautiful, Third the Most Sprightly.

INSPIRED BY INDIAN MUSIC.

The Director of the National Conservatory Adds a Masterpiece to Musical Literature.

MR. SEIDL LEADING THE NEW DVORAK SYMPHONY.

HERR ANTONIN DVORAK

FURTHER LISTENING

Symphony No. 8 in G, op. 88
This, the symphony which precedes the 'New World', is Dvořák's only other widely-popular symphony. It is deservedly popular because three of the four movements carry an astonishing abundance of ideas and freshly-wrought themes. It also marks the first time Dvořák was willing to experiment with the forms that carry all this invention. Consequently, the work has a more expansive and more natural air to its music-making, and benefits greatly by this. Only in the finale does the inventiveness flag and the buoyancy which lifts the rest of the work is replaced by something close to bombast.

Serenade for Strings, op. 22
Of the two Serenades Dvořák wrote, one for strings and the other for wind instruments, this string serenade is undoubtedly the more immediately attractive: its uninterrupted popularity since its first performance attests to that. But it also happens to be a superbly crafted piece of work, showing all Dvořák's normal melodic fertility and subtleties of scoring. It is a wholly delightful piece, all five movements containing gems of wit and invention, though perhaps nothing is more impressive than the beautiful sweep of the opening melody.

Rusalka
Dvořák's most successful and oft-revived opera is based on a rather grim Czech fairy tale. Launched on an enthusiastic public in 1901, it has remained a favourite in Czechoslovakia ever since, and its fame has spread through the opera-loving centres of Europe. It is a well-constructed work with considerable dramatic impact, enhanced by the composer's special gift for melodic invention for the human voice. The beautiful aria, *Invocation to the Moon,* sung by the heroine, Rusalka, is a much-performed concert piece which, like Puccini's greatest arias, stands equally successfully on its own.

String Quartet No. 1 in A Major
This is the first of Dvořák's works to contain a glimmer of nationalist feeling. Joyful and spontaneous, it displays a maturity lacking in his earlier work.

IN THE BACKGROUND

IN THE BACKGROUND

'Land of opportunity'

The America that greeted Dvořák was an exciting and ever-changing one. Brave and adventurous pioneers were pushing back the frontiers of the wild west, and a whole new world was opening up.

Peter Newark's Western Americana

Spurred on by hope and the determination to reach a land that promised freedom and endless opportunity, countless emigrants crossed the vast continent of America, heading west by wagon train.

The Granger Collection

When the first European settlers walked ashore the Atlantic coast of America at the beginning of the 17th century, their every step demarcated a new western frontier. And for the next 300 years their descendents pressed on inexorably, establishing frontier after frontier until that vast sprawling continent was finally subdued.

By the end of the Civil War in 1865 this process of westward expansion had gone a long way. Few could remember a time when the Mississippi River had been the natural as well as national boundary on the west, and beyond it to the Missouri River and southwest into Texas pioneer farmers had created thriving communities. Some 1500 miles further on, far across the mighty Rockies and warmed by the waters of the Pacific lay gold-rich California and its splendid new city San Francisco. All along the coast from British Columbia in the north to Mexico in the south an energetic race of adventurers was forcing the earth to yield its riches – most spectacularly so its mineral wealth, but there was an abundance of timber and agricultural wealth too.

Between these newly settled areas lay the final and most awesome frontier of all – the Great Plains. For long the Great Plains had stymied prospective settlers. It was a seemingly endless expanse of prairies, almost treeless and studded with bunch grass, scorched by sun and wind in summer and swept by blizzards in winter, where long stretches of killing drought were occasionally interrupted by torrential rains and hailstorms which could flatten a man. To the west these inhospitable prairies finally gave way to mighty mountains and canyons, majestic to behold, but the graveyard of many who had tried to struggle through them to reach fabled California. Through it all roamed bands of Indians, who had every reason to discourage yet one more intrusion on their shrinking homeland. Not for nothing was this whole region known in geography books of the time as the Great American Desert, or as Mark Twain put it, 'one prodigious graveyard'.

This then, was the setting for the great drama that was to be played out in a single generation following the Civil War: the taming of the American West.

Building the rails west

The years immediately following the Civil War were boom times in the victorious North. Crucially for the opening of the West, the railway industry was geared up for phenomenal expansion. The settled eastern part of the nation was already well served by the railway, and indeed the western fingers of this network probed very near the edge of the frontier from Texas north to Wisconsin. From there, however, transportation and all communication slowed to the pace of the horse. From the 1850s stagecoach services had been in operation, notably the Butterfield Overland Mail and the legendary Wells, Fargo & Co., but while these wonderfully cinematic four- and six-horse coaches competed bravely with terrain, distance and hostile Indians, they were really obsolete from the beginning. The technology and wealth were there to span the continent by rail.

The first of the great transcontinental lines was begun even as war raged, in 1863. One portion, then the Union Pacific, was laid westward from Omaha, Nebraska, while the other, the Central Pacific came eastward from Sacramento, California. As almost everywhere in the English-speaking world, the labour employed on the eastern section was mainly Irish. In the west, however, it was Chinese, an early indication of America's true geographical position in

Peter Newark's Western Americana

The long and treacherous assault course to their western destination cost the lives of many pioneer men, women and children. For those who survived the harsh weather conditions – from blizzards to droughts – there was always the terrifying prospect of being attacked by rampaging Indians (above).

In its heyday, the famous Wells, Fargo & Co. stage-coach service was an invaluable means of transportation and communication. But even in 1866, when this photograph (left) was taken, its days were numbered – work on the great transcontinental railroad had begun.

the world.

On 10 May 1869 the two lines met at Promontory Point, some fifty miles west of Ogden, Utah, and as the famous golden spike was driven in the telegraph tapped out the message that the United States was finally spanned from sea to sea.

The building of the first transcontinental railway was one of the outstanding engineering achievements anywhere to that time, and others followed quickly behind, the Northern Pacific, the Great Northern and tens of thousands of miles of smaller lines spreading out across the West. A daunting vista still, but perhaps not quite so implacably hostile as had been assumed.

Home on the range

In 1865 something like five million unbranded longhorn cattle roamed the Texas prairie. Fierce, rangy creatures, these wild cattle were descended from breeds introduced by the Spanish centuries earlier. To destitute ranchers returning from defeat in the Civil War, these cattle were a resource of obvious potential, since there was an insatiable demand for beef in the urban north and east. But the means of cashing in on that resource was tantalizingly out of reach. How could they get the cattle to the market? Arduous drives to the distant slaughterhouses of Cincinnati, St. Louis and Chicago reduced the cattle to a near valueless state on arrival, and while some ranchers attempted this most settled for slaughtering thousands of these longhorns simply for tallow and hide.

Then in 1867 the situation changed overnight. The Kansas Pacific Railroad was building west from Kansas City, and a sharp-witted Illinois cattle dealer

An historic and memorable moment when East met West at Promontory, Utah, on 10 May, 1869 (above). The trains of the Union Pacific and the Central Pacific moved forward until they touched – the United States of America had been spanned by rail.

The opening of the West brought prosperity to the white man, but for the American Indian it was the beginning of the end. With the new railroad crossing the Great Plains, more and more people ventured west to make a new life. En route, huge herds of buffalo were indiscriminately slaughtered for sport by travel-weary passengers (right) – and deprived the Indians of their life source of food, fuel and clothing.

named Joseph McCoy immediately realized the implications. Well to the west of established agricultural settlement but beside the newly laid tracks, he chose his spot: Abilene, 'a small dead place of about a dozen log huts'. There he built shipping pens large enough to hold 3000 head of cattle, a hotel and a livery stable. By the end of that year 35,000 head of cattle had been shipped out of the first of the legendary cowtowns, and 1.5 million were to follow over the next four years. The greatest cattle movement in history had begun, and with it the brief heyday of the quintessential American hero, the cowboy.

The popular image of the cowboy has been romanticised for so long now and in so many different ways that it is difficult to see through that image to the real cowboy himself. What was life actually like on the trail? One thing it was not was romantic. As one chronicler has put it:

There was no romance in getting up at four o'clock in the morning, eating dust behind the trail herd, swimming muddy and turbulent rivers, nor in doctoring screw worms, pulling stupid cows from bog holes, sweating in the heat of summer, and freezing in the cold of winter.

These, then, were the physical elements the cowboy contended with. On top of all that, he lived in constant fear of the dreaded stampede. The sudden rearing of a horse, the barking of a distant coyote, the rumble of thunder, the crack of lightning, anything could galvanize thousands of terrified cattle into blind action. The suddenness and the violence of a stampede would shake even the most sanguine cowboy. As one recalled:

Sometimes the herd might get completely out of control and scatter for a hundred miles. While I was looking at him, this steer leaped into the air, hit the ground with a heavy thud, and gave a grunt that sounded like that of a hog. That was the signal. The whole herd was up and going _ and headin' right for me. My horse gave a lunge, jerked loose from me, and was away. I barely had time to climb into an oak. It took us all night to round them up. When we got them quieted the next morning, we found ourselves six miles from camp.

Turning from the hazards of the trail to the day-to-day organization and workload, the key figure that emerges is the trail boss. It was he who assigned the men their duties, and would rise first in the morning to wake them. He would ride ahead to make sure of water supplies and to choose the place to stop for a midday meal. And of course, he was responsible not only for the safety of the cattle but for the men themselves, for tending their injuries and settling their disputes.

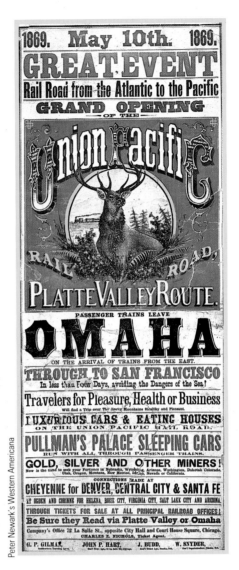

Advertising the event to beat all events, this poster (left), sums up the excitement stirred up by the 'grand opening' of the Union Pacific. No sooner had the famous golden spike been driven into the rails at Promontory Point than the maiden run from Omaha to San Francisco took place.

Some 20 years later, the accent was more on luxury than on adventure as can be seen by the advertisement for the 'Great Palace Reclining-chair Route' (far left).

Following breakfast at 3.30 in the morning the cowboys would take up their positions around the herd, and the day's drive would begin. Herds varied in size, but the norm was 2-3000 with each cowboy allocated about 300. The technique was to keep the cattle moving in a loosely controlled pack, at a pace that ensured both progress and calm. At 11 a.m., the entourage would come to a halt and the men fed, the cattle grazed and then settled down for a nap. Roused for the afternoon drive, the herd would start to pick up speed as the cattle began to thirst for their evening watering holes. By sundown they were content to settle, although occasionally during the night they would stand to stretch. The men on night watch were as vigilant as any sailor.

The next day, the same routine – with, as always, the imminent possibility of storm, stampede and Indian attack. The duration of the journey varied widely, depending on weather conditions as well as the starting and finishing points, but something like two months from Texas to Abilene was average.

Having survived the rigours of the trail, the cowboy finally found himself at one of the trail and rail junctions scattered across the Plains – dusty towns with names that are part of folklore like Witchita, Cheyenne, Abilene itself, and most famous of all, Dodge City, 'Queen of Cow Towns'. There he might visit a barbershop for a haircut and an overdue bath, then outfit himself with new boots and perhaps

a suit and hat. He would be careful, however, not to spend too much money on these preliminaries. For what he really wanted, and what the new cowtowns were well equipped to provide, was a few days' spree. Saloons, gambling halls, dance halls and brothels awaited his arrival with keen anticipation, and while cattle-brokers got on with the serious business of making money, he got on with the equally serious business of squandering it. The process rarely took long, however, and before he knew it the long trek back along the trail to Texas with another herd of longhorns began.

The mining bonanza

The discovery of gold in California in 1847 touched off the most feverish and famous 'rush' ever witnessed. But it was only the first of many fabulous strikes that turned the mountains of the American Far West into an Eldorado for fortune-seekers the world over. Next to California, the greatest of these strikes was the fabulous Comstock lode on the slopes of Mount Davidson in Nevada. Two Irish prospectors stumbled upon this unprecedently rich source of silver in 1859, and within a year the boisterous new town of Virginia City lay perched on the side of the mountain. A mining engineer's description of Virginia City in 1861 gives a fair indication of the conditions of life men will accept when bedazzled by the imminence of wealth.

Frame shanties pitched together as if by accident; tents of canvas, of blankets, of brush, of potato-sacks, and old shirts, with empty whisky barrels for chimneys; smoky hovels of mud and stone; coyote holes in the mountainside forcibly seized and held by men; pits and shafts with smoke issuing from every crevice; piles of goods and rubbish on craggy points, in the hollows, on the rocks, in the mud, in the snow, everywhere, scattered broadcast in pell-mell confusion, as if the clouds had burst overhead and rained down the dregs of all the flimsy, rickety, filthy little hovels and rubbish of merchandise that had ever undergone the process of evaporation from the earth since the days of Noah.

Over the next two decades major strikes of gold, silver and copper were made with wonderful regularity, and mining camps dotted the mountains and valleys from the Fraser River far to the north in British Columbia to Tombstone, on the edge of the Arizona Desert. Wherever they were, these mining camps, or mining towns as they became when the tents and shacks gave way to timber and brick buildings with false façades, were tough places – far tougher than the cattle towns further east. Many accounts are doubtless exaggerated: 'the roaring, raving drunkards of the bar-room, swilling fiery liquids from morning till night; the flaring and flaunting gambling-saloons, filled with desperados of

The lure of land ready for the taking brought many poor farming families out West. But life was tough for these homesteaders. Land was plentiful, but resources few and home was usually a simple cabin (above) made from the only building material available – prairie sod.

the vilest sort.' This is unlikely to be a description of the activities of all the inhabitants of Virginia City. But considering the fact that miners, unlike cowboys, were quite likely to have large sums of money about them when their luck was in it is not surprising that the lure of 'mining the miners' attracted as motley a crew of swindlers and cut-throats, thieves and whores as one could expect to encounter anywhere.

The pioneer on the plains
The cattle and mining kingdoms had an ephemeral, even vagrant quality about them, and they could never have claimed to 'tame' let alone settle the West. Only the establishment of settled farming communities could do that, and it was here that the westward urge came into the most direct conflict with the myth of the Great American Desert. It was one thing for free-spirited cowboys to endure the hardship of the open range, or for bold fortune-

A prominent figure in the 19th century western communities was the saloon owner (such as Jeff 'Soapy' Smith pictured above). Apart from a few 'good-time' girls, saloons were all-male enclaves and were often the only form of entertainment in town.

Roping a longhorn steer on the Texas prairie (right). The skill of the cowboy was constantly put to the test as keeping a herd under control was the only way to avoid the dreaded stampede.

seekers to put up with a few years in rowdy mining camps. It was quite another for young men and women, perhaps already with families, to carve out the stable, settled existence necessary for productive farming in the face of hostile conditions. Many thoughtful observers took the view that the Great Plains would never yield to settlement. The whole region, wrote Union General John Pope in 1866, 'is beyond the reach of agriculture, and must always remain a great uninhabited desert'.

At the same time, there were those who argued that the desert myth was precisely that, a myth, and that quite wonderful prospects lay in wait for those who were prepared to chance their arm. One traveller returned from northern Dakota to tell of soil 'of the richest sort and easily cultivated for there is neither stone nor stump to bother the plow'. A Kansas newspaper editor returned from a visit to the western part of that state in 1867 and waxed lyrical about an agricultural vista: 'rich as that on the banks of the far famed Nile . . .land before us, land behind us, land at the right hand, land at the left hand – acres, miles, leagues, townships, counties – oceans of land, all ready for the plough, good as the best in America, and yet lying without occupants.'

The truth lay somewhere in between such starkly contrasting views. Fertile land there was in abundance, and encouraged both by government and the new western railways, the final generation of

The real American cowboy (above) – dressed for the part, but here's where the resemblance to his celluloid counterpart ends – could tell a very different story about life on the trail: the workload, the danger and the harsh conditions that had to be endured as part of the job.

Fortunes were there to be made, but for many prospectors the only way to make a quick 'buck' was to try their luck at gambling (above) – a regular feature of saloon life.

American pioneers flooded onto the Great Plains in the years following the Civil War. But scanty rainfall and a climate of sometimes grotesque severity condemned these settlers to a life of toil and struggle – and for many the rewards were heartbreakingly meagre. It was particularly hard on the women. As farmers' wives they were used to the daily grind of domestic chores, but nothing back east had prepared them for the conditions on the plains. The hard water made washing almost impossible. During the long dry months of dust and wind the dust got every-where. It stung the eyes and got into the hair and stayed there. It crept through windows and covered the furniture the moment it was dusted. Many women, exhausted by fighting a losing battle, gave up the struggle against the dust and dirt and let their sod houses deteriorate into squalor.

Drought, and plagues of grasshoppers frequently reduced the pioneers to abject misery – and the brink of starvation. In 1874, this twin calamity struck

Peter Newark's Western Americana

with particular ferocity, and the nightmare quality of the grasshopper invasion was forcefully expressed by the editor of the Witchita City *Eagle:*

They came upon us in great numbers, in untold numbers, in clouds upon clouds, until their dark bodies covered everything green upon the earth . . .' A Kansas farmer, writing at the same time, wryly lamented, 'There has been no rain here of consequence for a couple of months, and between the drought, the cinch bugs and the grasshoppers we will be forced to go to Egypt or somewhere for our corn'.

In fact, most of these first pioneers stuck it out, and successive waves of settlers followed them – from Europe as well as the eastern states. Improved farming methods and new machinery succeeded in bringing almost the entire expanse of the Great Plains under cultivation, thereby providing one of the foundation stones of 20th-century America's prosperity.

The Indian tragedy

For all the hardships they faced on the Great Plains, the white newcomers were there by choice and could not, in a general sense, blame their plight on anyone else. For the Indians it was quite different. For centuries they had been pushed further and further west by the white man, and the Great Plains was their last stronghold. Taking into account those inhabiting the Rockies and the intermountain region they numbered about 250,000, with another 50,000 or so in the Indian Territory, later to become Oklahoma. But the salient point about the plains Indians – notably the Sioux, the Blackfeet, the Crow in the north, the Cheyenne of the central plains and the Apache and Comanche in the south – is that they were nomadic and extremely warlike.

The reason for this is that they were almost totally

As gold fever spread rapidly, prospectors, such as the three old timers pictured below, came from all over America in the hopes of striking it rich.

The last of the Apache chiefs, the legendary Geronimo (above). After surrendering in 1894, he brought the surviving members of his Chiricahua tribe to a reservation at Fort Sill in the northern part of Red River Country which is now Oklahoma. He died in 1909 still a prisoner of war.

Custer's Last Stand (right). Ignoring orders, and heavily outnumbered by Sioux, Cheyenne and Arapaho warriors, General George Armstrong Custer led his men into battle. All but a single horse were killed.

The Mansell Collection

Peter Newark's Western Americana

A group of Ute Indians (below). At first this aggressive Rocky Mountain tribe looked on the white man as an ally who could help drive the Cheyenne off the plains of Colorado. But, although they traded, trusted and even fought alongside the white man, in the end they too were forced off their land onto a reservation.

dependent on the American bison, or buffalo. They used its flesh for food, its hide for clothing, blankets, footwear and teepees, its horns for domestic implements like cups and spoons, and its bones for ornaments. Its sinews provided bowstrings and the stitching for garments, and even its dung, dried, was used for fuel. For thousands of years the plains Indians had hunted the buffalo on foot, but the introduction of the horse to the New World by the Spanish in the 16th century transformed their way of life. The horse provided the perfect answer to buffalo hunting, and within time the plains Indians became astonishingly skilful horsemen. They became fearsome warriors too, as their wide-ranging pursuit of

the great buffalo herds brought them into conflict with other tribes, similarly equipped with horses and that primitive, deadly weapon, the bow and arrow. Riding bareback at top speed they could slide down the side of the horse and cling on by a heel, leaving both hands free to fire a stream of arrows from beneath its neck.

Westward expansion after 1865 led inevitably to conflict between the whites and the Indians, indeed to a series of wars as the US Army moved west with the settlers in order to protect them. In the long run, all the advantages lay with the army, which was quite prepared to match savagery with savagery – and with interest. Ironically, however, the most celebrated engagement in the twenty years of bitter fighting that settled the issue was an Indian victory of shocking totality: the Battle of the Little Bighorn.

In June 1876, thousands of Sioux, Cheyenne and Arapaho were congregated along the Little Bighorn River in southern Montana. This gathering of the tribes for the annual sun dance, the Indians' most important religious ritual, was protected by an estimated 2500 warriors. Regardless, the Army was determined on a show of force in order to bring the Sioux and their mighty chief Sitting Bull to heel. Cavalry from all sides converged on the Indians.

Following a skirmish to the south of the Little Bighorn, Lieutenant George A Custer of the Seventh Cavalry was despatched with about 600 officers and men to locate the main body of the enemy. A vainglorious, reckless man if a courageous one, Custer blithely ignored his orders, which were simply to reconnoitre the area. Instead he drove his men as hard as he could right into the enemy camp. Then, ignoring their exhaustion, he mounted his fateful attack on 24th June. Despite being hopelessly outnumbered, he divided his force, which meant that he and his battalion, thought to have numbered 225, stood alone against an onslaught of whooping

warriors led by chiefs Gall, Crazy Horse and Two
Moons. Custer and his men were annihilated – and
this bungled venture became immortalized as
Custer's Last Stand.

Even such a victory – and it was by no means the
only mauling they inflicted on the army – only
prolonged the Indians' agony, and by the middle of
the 1880s their resistance had been crushed. The
West was finally 'safe', safe, that is, for the white man.
For the Indian, it marked his final, enduring tragedy.
One of the defeated chiefs summed up the despair of
a permanently eclipsed race; 'The white man made
us many promises, but he only kept but one. He said
he would take our lands, and he did.'

The western myth

In the census of 1900 it was stated that the frontier
no longer existed. There were by then approx-
imately half a million farms in Kansas, Nebraska, the
Dakotas and Oklahoma Territory, and a flourishing
cattle industry further to the west and north, as far as
the foothills of the Rockies. The rail network was
virtually complete, and with the Indian population
subjugated Americans could come and go as they
pleased, subject only to the normal hazards of life.
The Wild West was a thing of the past.

The idea of the West, or really a succession of
Wests, had always exercised a powerful hold on the
imagination of Americans – as a place of freedom
from constraint, of boundless opportunity and the
chance to start afresh, of adventure pure and simple.
The final disappearance of the frontier did not and
has not to this day removed the emotional appeal of
the West and what it stood for.

*The rapid growth, wealth and prosperity that came
with the opening up of America, can be seen clearly
in these two very different views of San Francisco
(above and below). In little over 40 years this gold-
rich Californian city had become every bit as
sophisticated as anywhere 'back East'.*

THE GREAT COMPOSERS

Edvard Grieg

1843–1907

Edvard Grieg's belief that the future of Norwegian music lay in a re-examination of its folk traditions helped to make him Norway's most celebrated composer. His spirited rhythms and fresh use of harmony captured the feel of the dance songs and ballads he was inspired by. Grieg chose to use simple constructions designed to show off his sense of melody. Memorable examples include Suites nos. 1 and 2 from his incidental music for Ibsen's Peer Gynt and his Piano concerto in A, both analysed in the Listener's Guide. His nationalistic music and settings helped re-kindle Norway's national pride as the nation moved toward independence, as In The Background *discusses. Grieg's genius in finding a musical equivalent to the spirit of the land and the people helped him to fulfil his desire to become a truly Norwegian composer.*

Edvard Grieg was born to a well-established family in Bergen and, on the insistence of the eccentric Ole Bull, was sent to the Leipzig Conservatory. A spirited, adventurous young man, he disliked the institutional nature of the Conservatory, but found greater happiness after leaving Leipzig for Copenhagen. A meeting with the nationalist composer Rikard Nordraak shaped his musical future; he became determined to celebrate Norway's folk traditions in music, returning to Norway to found the Norwegian Academy of Music in 1867. Accolades both at home and abroad for his melodic works included the admiration of Liszt. He toured Scandinavia, the Continent, and England, and in 1874 was awarded a yearly stipend by the government of Norway for his nationalist efforts, which he remained devoted to until his death in 1907.

'Lively Bergen fellow'

Ever genial and urbane, Edvard Grieg was the
first great Norwegian composer and his music
carried the beauty of his land to people all over

Edvard Grieg was born in the busy and prosperous fishing town of Bergen (right) in June 1843. His father, Alexander Grieg (left) a wealthy merchant of Scottish origin, was the British consul at Bergen. Grieg's mother, Gesine Judith Hagerup (left), a talented musician, was his first music teacher.

The turning point in Grieg's hitherto informal musical education came in 1858, when Ole Bull (below) – one of the most important figures in the creation of a nationalist school of music in Norway – heard the young Grieg play the piano. Bull insisted that his parents send him to the Leipzig Conservatoire 'to become a musician'.

Grieg was born in Bergen in June 1843 and died there in September 1907. For the composer who was to become the best loved and most celebrated in Norway's history, Bergen was a fitting birthplace. It was both a lively cultural centre and a prosperous commercial town, and Grieg's parentage reflects both these advantages. His father, Alexander Grieg, was a rich merchant of Scottish origin, and his mother, Gesine Judith Hagerup, was a gifted poet and musician from a famous Bergen family.

The town, sandwiched between the sea and a steep mountain range, alive with the to-ing and fro-ing of its sea traffic and buffetted by capricious weather, had nurtured the talents of some of Norway's finest dramatists, poets, painters and musicians. Grieg, on his 60th birthday, made a speech acknowledging the special debt he owed to his home town:

My material has been drawn from the whole of the surroundings of Bergen. Its natural beauty, the life of its people, the city's achievements and activities of every kind have been an inspiration to me. I find the odour of the German Quay exciting; in fact I am sure my music has a taste of codfish about it.

At the age of six, Grieg began piano lessons with his mother and made rapid progress. Gesine Grieg's love of the keyboard music of Mozart, Beethoven, Weber and Chopin, which she played often was effectively communicated to Edvard. For him, routine practice was a chore, although he stuck to it well enough. But he loved to spend hour upon hour experimenting alone, drawing his own sounds out of the piano. These were his first voyages of discovery into the world of harmony, and many years later, in an essay called *My First Success,* he recalled one of these childhood experiments:

First a third, then a chord of three notes, then a full chord of four, ending at last with both hands. Oh joy! a combination of five – the chord of the ninth!

Grieg's spirit of adventure was not confined to music and he soon developed an intense dislike for institutional life. When the time came for him to go to school in Bergen, he rebelled, but had to accept his fate. At school, of course, scorn was poured on his sensitive, wayward nature and his early experiments in music met with derision. From the age of ten on, he thought of the most incredible ways of escaping.

Grieg's longed-for escape from school finally came just before his 15th birthday. In the summer of 1858, the Griegs were visited by a remarkable man, the 'Paganini of the North' Ole Bull, perhaps the most famous man in Norway. Part genius, part charlatan, and charismatic eccentric, the violinist Ole Bull had become a folk hero, a symbol of the new Norway which had declared its independence half a century previously.

Edvard was asked to play for the distinguished guest. Bull was impressed and insisted that the boy be despatched to the Leipzig Conservatoire 'to become a musician'. In Leipzig, the finest piano masters in North East Europe were to be found. Grieg's parents were easily persuaded and, the following October, Grieg began the long journey to Leipzig, feeling 'like a parcel full of hopes'.

The young romantic

How those hopes were to be dashed! Leipzig turned out to be just as oppressive an institution for the boy from the north as school had been. Grieg's first teacher, Plaidy, far from allowing the young romantic to experiment, prescribed a strict diet of fiendish piano studies by such worthy, but unexciting composers as Clementi, Kuhlau and Czerny – all of whom Grieg 'loathed like the plague'. But Grieg was lucky enough to study under Ignaz Moscheles as well. The kindly Moscheles, who had been a close friend of Mendelssohn and a piano virtuoso in his own right, was far more liberal – although even he preferred Mozart to Chopin.

Yet the composition tutor, Reinecke, made him jump through some impossible hoops. How was he to attempt string quartet and symphonic writing when he had no prior experience? He struggled miserably with his assignments, too young at the time to realize that his was a lyric rather than epic talent which would flower in exquisite songs and piano miniatures, rather than vast romantic forms. Further despondency set in during the summer of 1860 when a serious attack of pleurisy struck, presaging the respiratory troubles which would trouble him for the rest of his life.

Although he claimed to have 'left the institution as stupid as I entered it', a very different impression is given by his teachers and fellow students. He had come to be known as 'that lively Bergen fellow, outspoken, quick-witted and enthusiastic.' Reinecke, especially, wrote of Grieg's 'significant musical talent, especially for composition', while one of his piano teachers, Hauptmann, called him 'an outstanding pianist and among the best of our students.' If nothing else, a period spent with access to public music making at the famous Leipzig Gewandhaus – where on one occasion Grieg heard Clara Schumann perform her husband's piano concerto – must have been a musical education in itself.

In 1862, Grieg put the mixed blessing of his Leipzig career behind him, as soon as his course finished, and went home to Norway to face the task of building a professional reputation. He began by giving a concert in Bergen, which included perform-

Grieg was 15 when he was enrolled as a student at the Leipzig Conservatoire (left). After a disappointing beginning with some indifferent tuition, he was taught by E. F. Wenzel, who had been a close friend of Schumann, and it was he who instilled in Grieg a deep love for Schumann's music. Before Grieg left the Conservatoire in 1862 one of his compositions (below), Vier Stücke (Four Pieces for Piano – dedicated to his teacher Wenzel) was performed at the students' examination.

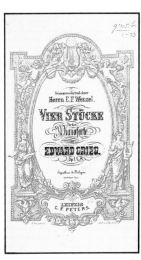

In 1863 Grieg left Bergen to live in Copenhagen (right). Although Norway was independent of Denmark, Copenhagen was still the centre for Norwegian cultural and intellectual life, and here Grieg began mixing with a circle of musicians and literary figures, including Hans Christian Andersen.

In 1864 Grieg became engaged to his cousin, Nina Hagerup. A talented singer, she was both the inspiration and best interpreter of Grieg's song songs, including 'I love thee' (above).

ances of studies by Moscheles, a sonata by Beethoven and three of his own *Four Piano Pieces,* Op. 1. The concert was very well received, although Grieg could hardly have foretold from this modest success that it marked the beginning of an internationally successful career as a concert pianist. That was for the future. In the meantime Grieg began to realize that it might not have been such a good idea to return to Norway so soon. The urge took him to go abroad again in search of fresh ideas and influences.

Copenhagen

Although Norway was tied to Sweden, the real melting pot of Norwegian intellectual and cultural life was still Copenhagen. Certainly for a composer in the making, a period of residence in the Danish capital was essential. So Grieg went to Copenhagen and immediately tried to engage the attention of two of the father figures of Scandinavian music. The leading Danish composer, Niels Gade, was hardly encouraging. J. P. E. Hartmann was much warmer and Hartmann's interest in Nordic legend was soon to inspire Grieg himself.

The three years Grieg spent in Copenhagen were a happy contrast to his term in Leipzig. He fell in with kindred spirits of his own generation, took pleasure in the stimulation of life in the capital, the idyllic gentleness of the surrounding countryside, the proximity of the sea – all providing a delightful setting for the leisurely life of a young artist whose personal life had just taken on a new and romantic dimension. Grieg had met his cousin, Nina Hagerup, another native of Bergen, who had spent most of her life in Denmark. They fell in love and became engaged in July 1864. As an engagement present Grieg wrote for Nina one of his most lyrical songs, *I Love thee,* setting verse by Hans Christian Anderson. From that time on, Nina's poetic sensitivity and enchanting voice were to be the inspiration for Grieg's songwriting.

Later that year, after returning from a summer holiday in Norway, visiting his parents and spending time with Ole Bull, Grieg experienced a new artistic awakening. It happened through the agency of a new friend, the 22-year-old Rikard Nordraak, to whom Bjornsen had paid the compliment, 'to be with him was a feast from beginning to end.' Grieg was immediately carried away by Nordraak's romantic and passionate belief in everything ethnically Norwegian – the sagas, the mountains, the fjords, the country people, and all. Nordraak bolstered Grieg's belief in the possibility of creating a true Norwegian nationalism in music and, together with a group of other musicians, they founded a society called Euterpe, which put on concerts of contemporary Scandinavian music.

The friendship between Grieg and Nordraak deepened and they cemented it by a firm pact to make it their lives' work to express in music the spirit of Norway and bring to fulfilment the work Ole Bull had begun. Sadly, their pact was to be broken by Nordraak's premature death only two years after their first meeting, but this, if anything, intensified in Grieg the zeal to raise the musical consciousness of Norway.

Return to Norway

Grieg's artistic mission was clear, but he delayed taking up residence in Norway to travel more widely in Europe. He and Nordraak had dreamed of Italy but Nordraak's fast declining health made it impossible

Grieg became a close friend of Rikard Nordraak (right), whom he met in Copenhagen in 1864-65. Nordraak, then aged 22, was the central focus of a movement to establish a school of Norwegian nationalist music. Grieg, inspired by Nordraak's enthusiasm for all things Norwegian, made a pact with Nordraak to express in music the spirit of Norway. This was broken by the premature death of Nordraak two years after their first meeting. Grieg, however, continued on what he saw as his true path – that of becoming a Romantic Nationalist composer. Prior to meeting Nordraak Grieg had spent the summer renewing his love for the Norwegian countryside (below).

for him to travel. Leaving his friend in the throes of tuberculosis, Grieg set out for Italy on his own.

He travelled widely, sightseeing in Rome, Naples, Capri, and Sorrento. He visited the archeological findings at Pompeii and heard 'appalling music in the Chiesa Nuova: Bellini, Donizett, Rossini!' He met a galaxy of cultural stars, was mildy scandalized by the sight of Liszt in philandering mood and Ibsen under the influence of the local wine. The one shadow cast on Grieg's Italian trip was the grief he felt upon receiving news of Nordraak's death. In his diary he noted the date with a black cross, and later that day he began to write a moving tribute to his friend, *Funeral March in Memory of Richard Nordraak.* He wrote a letter of sympathy to Nordraak's father expressing the determination within him to keep to the task they had assigned themselves:

his cause should be my cause, his goal mine. Do not believe that what he aspired to will be forgotten. ...

Now determined to carve a future for Norwegian music on his own, Grieg returned to Norway to make a base in Christiania. At first, the capital city was unwelcoming and it seemed impossible to find a permanent job. He plucked up the courage to ask Ibsen to use his influence with Bjørnsen – Director of the Christiania Theatre – to persuade him to appoint the young composer to the vacant position of music director there. Disappointingly, Bjørnsen failed to respond.

In the face of such indifference, Greig decided to take his future into his own hands. On 15 October 1866, he managed to obtain a public concert with an all-Norwegian programme. Incredibly, this was an historic event in itself. Nina sang some songs by Nordraak, and, out of Grieg's portfolio came several songs with words by Hans Christian Andersen, some

piano music and his first violin sonata. Thanks to a generous article in a Christiania daily newspaper – written by the composer Otto Winter-Hjelm, the first Norwegian to compose a symphony – entitled *On Norwegian Music and Some Compositions by Edvard Grieg'*, the concert was well attended, and finally turned out to be a commercial as well as an artistic success. Certainly it established Grieg as the bright new star of Norwegian contemporary music. He soon began to attract pupils and accepted an invitation to become the conductor of the city's orchestral society, the Harmoniske Selskab. Then, with the help of O. Winther Hjelm, Grieg launched the Norwegian Academy of Music in January 1867. It was an encouraging start.

The blissful summer

The following June, Grieg and Nina Hagerup were married. On 10th April 1868, Nina gave birth to their daughter, Alexandra. The Griegs spent a blissful summer in a rented cottage in Denmark. It was during these warm, happy days that Grieg conceived the work that to this day is a symbol of Norwegian

Nordraak's enthusiasm for the traditional elements of Norwegian life stimulated a similar passion in Grieg. Amongst other things Grieg was overwhelmed by the beauty of folk costumes (above) and by the simplicity of peasant life (above right).

romanticism, the Piano Concerto in A minor.

Yet despite this creative flowering, and his popularity in Christiania, Grieg was still far from achieving the widespread recognition he believed he deserved. Christiania was still very much a musical backwater. Grieg was itching for a new move. Then, in late 1868, he received a charming letter from Franz Liszt, praising his violin sonata (opus 8) in his most elegant French, and adding, 'I cordially invite you to come and stay for a while in Weimar so that we may have the opportunity of getting to know one another better.'

Unfortunately, Grieg could not immediately set out for Weimar, much though he wanted to. First the new concerto had to be premiéred in Denmark and at home, followed by the summer vacation period at Grieg's family estate at Landås.

While he was at Landås, Grieg made a very significant discovery for the future direction of his career. He found a book of Norwegian folk music, *'Older and Newer Mountain Melodies'*, compiled by the organist Ludvig Lindemann, who over 25 years had amassed a collection of melodies from folk fiddlers and singers in the more isolated parts of Norway. Grieg began to appreciate for the first time the boundless wealth and diversity of his native traditional music, and at last he saw how he could incorporate folk music into his own art. He soon set to work at his own arrangements of Lindemann's tunes, dedicating the first collection to Ole Bull. From that time onwards, he was continually indebted to Lindemann's collection for new ideas.

Liszt and 'Peer Gynt'

At last, in February 1870, Grieg finally managed to visit Liszt – but in Rome, not Weimar. Grieg sent animated letters home telling how 'the Maestro' seized upon his portfolio and pulled out the G major sonata for violin and piano. There then ensued one of Liszt's remarkable feats of sight-reading. He played

the sonata through at sight, playing both piano and violin parts, with a perfect understanding of all the composer's intentions and with all the nuances and effects. Liszt disdained compliments, saying, 'I am an experienced musician and ought to be able to play at sight.' At another meeting, Liszt played the A minor piano concerto and his enthusiasm was impressive to behold. After playing the work through, again at sight, Liszt went back to the piano and played the ending again. Finally he said, in a strange emotional way, 'Keep on, I tell you. You have what is needed and don't let them frighten you.'

Liszt's admiration won immense prestige for Grieg at home. In 1874, a letter arrived which was to commission from Grieg his most famous work; it came from Ibsen requesting incidental music to his bewitching drama *Peer Gynt.*

At first Grieg had immense difficulty putting his mind to the task. He admired *Peer Gynt* as a literary work but thought it 'the most unmusical of all subjects' and it took him many months to finish the 22 movements that went to making up the *Peer Gynt* score. It was February 1876 by the time the weighty score was finished and the production went ahead, strangely enough, in the absence of both the dramatist and the composer. It was a success, running for 37 performances and only closing because the Christiania theatre was destroyed by fire. But Ibsen, who did not get round to seeing the play until a future production, was only fairly satisfied – though

While holidaying in 1869 on the family estate at Landås Grieg discovered a copy of 'Older and Newer Mountain Melodies' (above) compiled by an organist, Ludvig Lindemann. The collection of melodies of the more remote parts of Norway made Grieg increasingly aware of the boundless wealth of his native music.

In 1876 Grieg and a friend, John Paulsen, went to Bayreuth for the first complete performance of Wagner's Ring. Grieg was asked by a local Bergen newspaper to send back reviews. Of Götterdämmerung, a scene from which is shown left, he wrote: 'I can hardly venture to write about the music of this last gigantic work. It presents such a world of greatness and beauty that one is almost dazzled.'

Grieg's relationship with the dramatist Henrik Ibsen (heavily caricatured right) dated from 1874, when he wrote the music for Ibsen's Peer Gynt.

From the summer of 1877 until late in the autumn of 1888, the Griegs rented accommodation in the beautiful countryside of Hardanger. First they stayed on a farm, then they took a guest house owned by friends in Loftus (left). During this stay Grieg experienced one of the most creative periods of his life, producing among other things one of his finest works, The Mountain Thrall, for solo baritone, two horns and strings.

In 1885 Grieg and his family moved to the house that had been built for them in the Westland, at Troldhaugen. He lived there for the next 20 years and his life fell into a fairly regular pattern of composition, walking tours and concert-giving. He is photographed below in front of his house in 1903, with his friend, Bjørnsterne Bjørson, one of the most influential literary and political figures of the day.

he admitted that Grieg's music made the heavy, sophisticated drama much more accessible to the public.

A hut by the fjord

With the onset of summer 1877, the Griegs began a 14 month stay in the beautiful Hardanger country, at first on a farm, then at Lofthus, in a guest house owned by some friends. Grieg, who insisted on absolute peace while he was composing, moved into a little hut on the edge of the fjord, just big enough to hold a piano, a table and chair, and affording a spectacular view of the glacier above. Unfortunately the sound of the piano tended to attract passers by. Grieg became more and more annoyed. So one day, he laid on vast quantities of food and drink and persuaded 50 local men to carry the piano, hut and all down the road to a more secluded spot. In a letter, Grieg tells how the operation went:

Now, 'troops' were sent to do the job and after a short while they came galloping at full speed with the heavy case as if it were filled with feathers.

At Hardanger, Grieg found a rich creative vein. In the peace of his newly-positioned hut, he wrote a string quartet, some choral music and one of his finest works – *The Mountain Thrall* for solo baritone, two horns and strings, which is based on an old Nor-

wegian ballad. It was given a prestigious first performance, in the presence of royalty, in the spring of the following year at Copenhagen. A masterpiece of national romanticism, it was declared by Grieg to have been written with his heart's blood.

The 1880s ushered in a fever of touring interspersed with periods of tranquility at Lofthus. Grieg's expanding reputation abroad meant that his autumn and winter months were generally filled with extended concert tours. One Herculean stint included visits to Weimar, Dresden, Leipzig, Meiningen, Breslau, Cologne, Karlsruhe, Frankfurt-am-Main, Arnhem, the Hague, Rotterdam, and Amsterdam! No wonder by the end of the year Grieg was so exhausted he had to refuse invitations to extend the tour still further.

A home at Troldhaugen

By now Grieg had decided to settle permanently in the Westland and began building the beautiful house at Troldhaugen that was to be his permanent home for the rest of his life. In 1885, the Grieg's took up residence in Troldhaugen and for the next twenty years Grieg's life conformed to a fairly regular pattern. The spring and early summer would be a time for composition, the later summer for mountain walking tours with friends, and then, come the autumn, back on to the concert schedule again, which, despite encroaching ill health, Grieg found so hard to resist.

Grieg began to be showered with distinctions from academic institutions all over Europe, including honorary doctorates from Oxford and Cambridge Universities, and Membership of the Institut de France. He was even made a Knight of the Order of Orange-Nassau, a distinction he accepted gladly, because, ever pragmatic as he wrote to a friend, 'orders and medals are most useful to me in the top layer of my trunk. The customs officials are always so kind to me at the sight of them.'

The Bergen festival

In 1898, an exciting event in Bergen provided Grieg with a wonderful opportunity. The town of Bergen had organized an exhibition of Norwegian arts, crafts and trade, to accompany a fishing congress that was planned for the summer. Grieg was invited to run a festival of Norwegian music at the same time. He did not hesitate to accept although a letter written to his friend Rontgen gives the impression that he might have repented at leisure:

The music festival is making my hair whiter than ever! The most incredible composers are arising out of the dark abyss and demanding in peremptory tone to be considered . . .

But in the end, as Grieg said himself, 'a lucky star reigned over the festival.' He kept performances of his own works to minimum, allowing such composers as Svensden, Selmer, Sinding, Nordraak and many others, to have their voice. For Grieg, the best reward was the sight of the audiences of country folk sitting 'as reverently as if they were in church, while the tears ran unchecked down their faces.' It was a great triumph and for Grieg represented the summit

of his career and the realization of his earlier ambition to become a truly Norwegian composer.

In the early years of the new century Grieg's health, never robust, began to seriously deteriorate. Refusing to read the danger signals, he allowed his concert tours to take him as far afield as Prague, Warsaw and Paris.

In the summer of 1906 Grieg wrote what was to be his last work, *Fire salmer* (Four Psalms) which was inspired by folk melodies.

The last year

Finding that the climate of Troldhaugen was adversely affecting his lungs, Grieg grudgingly moved into a Christiania hotel during the winter months of 1906-1907, which were to usher in the last year of his life.

The following summer, an urgent invitation arrived from the Leeds Festival begging Grieg to participate. Against all advice he accepted, but, as he was about to begin the journey to England, a sudden heart attack forced him into hospital in Bergen. On arrival he said: 'This, then, is the end.' Overnight he died in his sleep.

His body lay in state as thousands of compatriots, foreign dignatories and representatives of the musical world filed past to pay their respects. He was given a spectacular state funeral befitting a national hero, and the urn containing his ashes was placed in a recess cut from bare rock overlooking his favourite view of the fjord at Troldhaugen. It bore no epitaph, although Grieg's own words would have served:

Artists like Bach and Beethoven erected churches and temples on the heights. I only wanted . . . to build dwellings for men in which they might feel happy and at home!

Grieg moved away from Troldhaugen in the last months of his life because of ill-health. He died in September 1907 in Bergen, just before he was due to set off for England. In April 1908 his ashes were placed in a carved recess in the rock overlooking his favourite view of Troldhaugen. When she died in 1935, Nina's ashes were also placed there.

Björnson og Grieg. Troldhaugen 1903.

Orchestral works

Grieg's delicate mastery of the miniature form was given full expression in both Peer Gynt and the Piano Concerto in A – pieces made memorable by their simply constructed yet dramatic musical ideas.

Great works of art are rarely created without stress, but the difficulties surrounding Grieg's music for the Ibsen play, *Peer Gynt* were so fraught that it is a wonder it survived or even appeared in the first place. Grieg admired Ibsen's work but did not think *Peer Gynt* a suitable subject to set to music. Ibsen was not entirely happy about the music but conceded that it made the play more approachable. Today, critics agree that the music totally misrepresents the spirit of the drama.

Peer Gynt, a folk anti-hero who may actually have existed, is, in Ibsen's play, a self-willed, irresponsible peasant, quite unable to control his reckless and boastful tongue. His hyperactive imagination repeatedly lands him in trouble and those who meet him usually regret the encounter. A brief outline gives some idea of symbolism and fantasy involved.

Peer Gynt arrives uninvited at Haegstad farm, for the wedding celebrations of Ingrid, an old flame. He meets a beautiful maiden, Solveig, and tries to impress her with his extravagant lies. The other guests ridicule him and in a fit of vengeful pique he abducts Ingrid, later abandoning her in the forest. The villagers pursue him in vain and, after a number of escapades, he finds himself confronted by the horrific Mountain King of the Trolls — who reckons Peer would make an excellent son-in-law! Expressing thinly disguised contempt for the quality of the Trolls' music and dancing, Peer once more has to flee for his life. Peer eventually finds peace and safety deep in the forest; he builds himself a makeshift hut, is joined by Solveig and their love blooms.

After the death of his mother Åse, the irrepressible Peer deserts Solveig and goes in search of adventure. He ends up in the Arabian desert, where he finds a nobleman's clothes and magnificent steed which have been abandoned by thieves. Peer dresses himself in the grand clothes and rides to an oasis, where he is mistaken for a prophet by the local sheik and honoured with a dance. Anitra, one of the Arab girls, spies his riches and, dancing before him, she sets out to seduce the stranger. Both profit from the encounter; Peer is readily seduced and Anitra makes off with the gold and jewels.

The years pass. Solveig waits faithfully at home for Peer's return. At last, he returns to the forest and happens upon the old hut he had built so many years before. Inside, Solveig is singing. It is too much for Peer: he turns away in grief and guilt and runs into the forest. Even the trees and wind accuse him of wasting his life and in one of the wierdest scenes of all, he meets a button-moulder who has been sent to melt him down, for that is all Peer Gynt's life is worth — a button. Peer pleads for time to find someone who will defend him, but there is no-one. He turns instead to religion and in this way is granted a little extra time.

Solveig, now old and blind, leaves her hut to go to church. Peer is there, home at last, his long and inconsequential life nearly at an end. She takes him in her arms and sings him to sleep. In the background, ominously, the button-moulder is waiting, as the story ends.

Programme notes

The play *Peer Gynt* was written in Italy in 1867 and published the same year. It met with great success in Scandinavia, in spite of, or because of its harsh images and Nordic severity. In a long letter to Grieg, dated January 1874, Ibsen proposed that

A. O. Lamplough 'Evening at Edwa'. Mathaf Gallery, Motcomb St., London SW1

In 1874, the great dramatist Henrik Ibsen (below) asked Grieg to write the incidental music for his play Peer Gynt. Flattered by the invitation, Grieg threw himself into the project. However, the collaboration of two of Norway's greatest artists was not to be without its problems. Grieg found Peer Gynt 'a terribly unmanageable subject', and Ibsen was not exactly enthusiastic about Grieg's music. Nevertheless, the production proved a success, both at home and abroad. Edvard Munch's poster for the 1896 Paris production is shown, left.

Much of the charm of Grieg's music to Peer Gynt lies in its mingling of national colour with exotic locales. Morning Mood finds our unlikely hero in North Africa, watching the dawn rise over the desert sands (left).

the play would benefit from musical additions. Grieg was flattered but declared that he could hardly imagine anything less suitable for musical setting. Nevertheless, he set aside his current projects, thinking that Ibsen required only a few fragments of music – even though Ibsen's letter expressly called for a substantial score, including a large-scale tone poem that was in fact never composed. The score was finished in September 1875 and the performance was duly given in Christiania (now Oslo) on 24 February 1876. Both Ibsen and Grieg missed the opening night; the former was abroad and the latter was in Bergen. It was, however, a great success and a run of 37 performances was only terminated when fire destroyed the costumes and scenery.

In 1886 a publisher offered to bring out the music separately but Grieg was so diffident about its viability, both outside the theatre and outside Scandinavia, that he insisted on making a four-movement suite (1888) in which the order of the movements bore no relation to the drama. A second suite, at first including the Dance of the Troll King's Daughter, appeared in 1891.

Later still, an Oslo theatre demanded yet more music: by now the entire score ran to more than 20 movements, but the two suites represent, if not the essence of the play, certainly the best of Grieg. In the

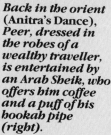

Back in the orient (Anitra's Dance), Peer, dressed in the robes of a wealthy traveller, is entertained by an Arab Sheik, who offers him coffee and a puff of his hookah pipe (right).

Åse's Death an episode of touching sadness, depicts the dying moments of Peer's mother. Using only muted strings, Grieg conjures up the quiet, mournful atmosphere (left). As the music fades into silence, the old lady's life finally ebbs away.

following notes, the numbers refer to the position of each movement in the complete score.

Suite no. 1

Morning Mood (no. 19)
This is the Prelude to Act IV of the drama. Peer Gynt is in North Africa watching the sun rise over the Sahara Desert. The opening flute melody is embellished with tiny gracenotes, as if heard against a sparse background of birdsong. Oboe takes up the melody and the two instruments alternate until strings swell and extend the melody as the sun breaks over the bleak horizon and Grieg expertly catches the languid atmosphere of the sun's rays warming the endless sand.

Åse's Death (no. 18)
Peer's mother, Åse, lies dying. The fugitive

son sits with her and together they recall happy and sad times as she fades peacefully away. This intense miniature for muted strings alone is constructed entirely of a simple musical idea:

Example 1

For a moment, the old lady's memories are strong and confident, but Grieg turns the theme upside down and its drooping phrases reflect her failing strength. He marks the last note *morendo* – dying away.

Anitra's Dance (no. 22)
The scene is a tent by a desert oasis. Peer, taken for a wandering nobleman, is entertained with coffee and a hookah pipe proffered by an Arab Sheik – and to his even greater delight, by the inevitable dancing

girls. *Their* full dance is heard in Suite no. 2; what we hear now is the dance of just one of the girls, Anitra, who has her mind on Peer's money. With bland disregard for geographical viability, she dances a solo mazurka. Its seductive grace so captivates Peer that the last thing on his mind is where this native girl learnt the steps of a Polish dance! With muted strings and the glint of triangle, Grieg perfectly conveys the half-lit intimacy of the scene and, in the middle section, the soaring cellos hint at Peer's burgeoning desire for the exotic maiden.

In the Hall of the Mountain King (no. 9)
In the Norwegian mountains, Peer flirts with a strange woman, dressed in green, spinning fabulous yarns and eventually learning to his dismay that she is none other than the daughter of the Troll King. After all his bombast, he must meet her

Lured into the **Hall of the Mountain King** *by the Troll King's daughter, Peer finds himself living the most hideous nightmare. Grotesque creatures (left) press round him, threatening to engulf him, their taunts and jibes rising to shrieks of 'Kill him!'. The music takes on their crudeness and barbarity – growing louder and louder as Peer's terror mounts. This is the most famous episode in* Peer Gynt, *although the composer himself described it as 'full of cow-pats'.*

father. He stands awkwardly in the hall, amid grotesque, supernatural folk who press about him like malodourous vermin and who soon realize he is a mere mortal.

'Cow pats' is how Grieg described this music, 'full of self-satisfied ultra-Norwegianism'. He detested the piece, excusing himself for having written it by explaining that its grotesque tune for bassoons, menacing sneers from muted horns and gradual increase in volume and speed were an ironic jibe at the excessive nationalism of 'certain colleagues'. The movement is, in fact, a miniature masterpiece of its kind, depicting a slow change from Peer's horrified fascination in his surroundings to sheer terror as 'a sticky mass of hair and snouts' (to quote a recent commentator) hound him round the hall of the Troll King and unearthly voices come at him from sides shrieking 'Kill him! Kill him!'

Suite no. 2

Abduction (Ingrid's Lament) (No. 5)

In Act I of the drama, Peer Gynt gatecrashes a wedding and lets his tongue run riot in a series of brash tales. The guests taunt him as an irresponsible liar; in fury he seizes the bride, Ingrid, and rushes her off into the forest. This Prelude to Act II is, by turns, ferocious and pleading. The distraught girl's ineffectual struggles and her heartfelt entreaties for release are all in vain. Peer keeps her captive all night and in the morning abandons her, lost and alone in the forest.

Arab Dance (no. 21)

If *Morning Mood* and *Anitra's Dance* fail to convey in musical terms the Arabian scene of the action, *Arab Dance* certainly makes amends with its effective display of exotic orientalism. So-called 'Turkish'

instruments (triangle, cymbals, bass drum) are prominent – they are heard at the beginning and the bass drum has the last word – and the percussion is further enriched by two types of tambourine. Two piccolos begin the dance:

Example 2

2 piccolos
(sounding one octave higher)

In the stage version, the dancing girls sing that a noble lord has come to them from across the sea of sand. 'Play the flute, sound the drum! The Prophet has come, The Prophet has come.'

In the central section Anitra (whose part is taken by violins), sings a blatantly flattering song of the stranger's influence and might – but also of his gold and diamonds. Evidently, Anitra has her priorities straight and her strategy well worked out. The

Danby 'Love deceived' (detail). The Victoria and Albert Museum, Bulloz

In the Abduction *scene, Peer snatches a young bride from a wedding and makes off with her into the forest. The next day he abandons her, leaving the poor, distraught girl to lament her fate (right).*

worldly Peer could not resist her, even if he wanted to!

Peer Gynt's Homecoming (no. 26)

As the tale nears its end, Peer (now an old man) is returning home his beard and white hair blowing in the wind as he stands in the bow of the ship but his adventures are far from over. As a prelude to Act V, Grieg wrote a splendid tone poem full of bracing northern sea winds and the slap of sail on rigging. A storm approaches. If the flute motive that depicts the raging wind owes something to Beethoven's 'Pastoral' Symphony, this does nothing to detract from the power of the movement. Prancing brass and swirling strings drive the boat along before the gale, as thunder and lightning play all about. In the drama, the ship is driven on to rocks and founders but, for the concert suite, Grieg lets the storm blow itself out, linking it more effectively with the last movement.

Solveig's Song (no. 17)

This meltingly lovely melody, based on a Norwegian folk song, is heard several times in the stage version. The fugitive Peer has built a hut in the forest; Solveig comes to him through the snow. After an introduction on muted strings, harp and horns strum and accompaniment to the song itself. It is a sweetly sad song, the epitome of Grieg's gentle art and, as it slips from A minor to A major ('very softly' requests the composer), it seems to recall some of the most magical moments in Schubert. At the end, the introduction returns, as if drawing a delicate veil over the entire suite.

Piano Concerto in A minor

The Piano Concerto was written at a happy and rewarding time for Grieg. In June 1867 he married his cousin, Nina Hagerup, and he had recently been involved in the formation of a society for the propagation of Scandinavian music. A co-founder of the society, the composer Rikard Nordraak (who died at the tragically early age of 23) fervently believed that the future of Norwegian music lay in a study of its folk traditions. He made a profound impression on Grieg, who wrote of their first meeting: 'I will never forget it. Suddenly a mist fell from my eyes and I knew the way I had to take. It was not precisely Nordraak's way, but I realized that the way for me passed through him'. From then on, Grieg became a nationalist composer, and evidence of his new-found awareness of his national heritage is to be heard in the Piano Concerto. The piece was written while Grieg and his wife were holidaying in Sollerød (in Denmark) in 1868, and the first publication appeared in 1872.

Programme notes

On publication in 1872, the Concerto was an immediate success. Not least because its nationalism, which might have offended listeners in those unenlightened times, was partly buried in the international and popular nature of the music. Despite it popularity Grieg himself was dissatisfied with the piece and constantly made revisions to it. A miniaturist at heart, he disdained the earnestly-argued symphonic style of, among others, Brahms and contented himself with a simple structure designed to show off his unique melodic genius.

First movement: Allegro molto moderato

The movement begins with one of the most striking gambits in music: a brief and compelling drum roll *crescendo* (very quiet to very loud), a sharp chord for full orchestra and a precipitate tumble in a series of rising phrases; then woodwind and horn announce a marchlike theme that

The exotic **Arab Dance** *prepares us for the seduction scene to follow. The scheming dancing girl, Anitra, takes the floor (below), and soon has Peer exactly where she wants him!*

Gérôme 'Dance of the Almeh'. Dayton Institute. Christopher Barker

Understanding music: incidental music

Music and drama have often combined at many different levels. At one end of the scale is the fusion we know as opera while, at the other, are overtures and *entr'actes* – pieces performed quite independently of the dramatic action. In between come all the songs, dances, marches and lavish musical entertainments which are performed in the course of a play. The term 'incidental music' usually refers to any combination of these elements which, however relevant and important to the drama, do not form the major part of it.

The precedent for including music in dramatic productions goes back at least to the ancient Greeks. Although it now seems unlikely that the tragedies of Euripedes or his contemporaries were declaimed to music throughout (a theory which at the end of the 16th century led to the development of opera), they certainly used music to accompany entrances and exits and some of the chorus passages would have been chanted in procession. In medieval drama too, music played an important part, particularly in drawing attention to special effects such as the ever-popular moment of divine intervention. During the 16th century, the place of incidental music as we understand it today became more clearly defined, at first in Italian comedies, where the *'intermedii'* – musical entertainments performed between acts – eventually became self-contained works in their own right. At this time, musical interpolation was considered more appropriate to comedy than to tragedy; musical numbers often took the form of choruses of nymphs and shepherds or satyrs, and these would have been rather incongruous placed within the lofty verses and sustained tension of tragic drama. A notable exception occurred in Shakespeare – with Ophelia's songs in *Hamlet* and Desdemona's Willow Song in *Othello*.

The growth of incidental music in spoken plays was, however, overtaken by that of opera and its greater scope for composers with theatrical inclinations. The one tradition that continued was the provision of fresh musical settings for Shakespeare productions. It was this tradition that prompted Goethe and Schiller to provide similar pieces in their dramas. Perhaps the most famous incidental music for a Goethe play is Beethoven's contribution to *Egmont*. Unlike those of his predecessors, Beethoven's score was intimately related to the action of the play, with the overture setting the mood and foreshadowing the final victory of the ending.

Mendelssohn's music to Shakespeare's **A Midsummer Night's Dream** *(above) lives on quite independently of the play as a favourite concert piece.*

The partnership of Goethe and Beethoven was clearly one of equals. On other occasions, less distinguished plays were provided with music of a far superior quality – hence Helmina von Chezy's *Rosamunde von Cypern* has vanished without trace, while Schubert's *Rosamunde* lives on. Indeed, the incidental music of the Romantic era is almost always heard in the concert hall but not the theatre. Performances of *A Midsummer Night's Dream* and Mendelssohn's idyllic music or Ibsen's *Peer Gynt* with Grieg's work are a rarity indeed, although both have an assured independent existence.

As the 19th century progressed, the relationship between literature and music became closer and a glance through the works of many Romantic composers reveals numerous familiar dramatic titles. Many of these pieces were never intended for the theatre and belong instead to the genre of programme music – works like Tchaikovsky's 'Romeo and Juliet' or Strauss's *Macbeth,* for example, tell their own distinctive stories.

Since the first World War, the provision of incidental music in the theatre has waned, partly for economic reasons, partly because the trend has been towards simple, stark productions. Opportunities for composers have, on the other hand, been greatly extended in the area of music for films and television. American composers who were pioneers in the art of writing music for motion pictures included Virgil Thomson, Marc Blitzstein, and Aaron Copland, who won an Academy Award for his original score for *The Heiress* in 1948.

Noel Paton 'Midsummer Night's Dream' (detail) AKG

quickly smoothes into a rising continuation on clarinet and bassoon (featuring a triplet).

Example 3

[musical notation]
clarinets(with bassoons)

This triplet, (three notes played in the space of two), provides a little 'kick' to the rhythm and is a device much loved by romantic composers — mostly because it so easily suggests a subtle quickening of the pulse or, say, a feeling of stress or yearning.

The theme flowers briefly but yields temporarily to the marchlike idea, now played by the soloist. A tripping dance then enters, taking the soloist high into the upper reaches of the keyboard from which he descends in a graceful cascade of notes. A brief linking passage changes the mood to one of serene contemplation as cellos sing a new melody, now punctuated delicately by downward three-note phrases from flute and clarinet. Our friend the triplet can be heard in the cello melody; and in, the passage that follows, the three notes become five. Then, as the tune bares

In the elegiac Adagio, Grieg blends his instinctive romanticism with a love of his homeland's native scenery (below).

The first movement of Grieg's Piano Concerto is filled with an unmistakeable passion and tension. Its stressful mood is reflected in Munch's woodcut (right) where two lovers stand alone, unable to bridge the gulf between them.

its passionate heart, the triplet takes charge, infusing the music with an unmistakable feeling of stress.

Now, for the first time, since the opening chord, the whole orchestra (except timpani) is involved. It plays an animated passage which echoes the Norwegian mood of *Peer Gynt*. The passage ends with a glorious fanfare for trumpets, before dissolving into the familiar march tune, now played gently by flute, then horn, over a rippling piano accompaniment.

A more severe announcement of the march, on brass and strings, is answered consolingly by the soloist and a further statement forces the pianist to respond with a reminiscence of the opening tumble down the keyboard. The time for a full recapitulation has arrived and the music is repeated with minor — but interesting — changes. The cello melody once again brings an excited series of triplets, and leads to a sustained chord.

A brilliant piano cadenza deals mainly

Example 4

Munch 'The Lonely Ones' Oslo Kommunes Kunstsamlinger, Munch-Museet

with the march, at one point interspersing it with mightly roaring runs in the lower part of the keyboard before moving on. Eventually, with strings of *tremelos* (rapid, repeated notes), the orchestra joins in and the movement looks set to end in subdued mood. But suddenly, as if the sun had emerged from behind a cloud, the mood of the movement changes and it is transformed into a joyous and light-hearted dancing affair. The movement ends, as it began, with a strikingly brilliant solo flourish from the piano.

Second movement: Adagio
At first it would seem that the slow movement is to be a study in contrasting themes: the strings – in that curiously nasal quality imparted by mutes – play an elegiac melody in D flat, embellished by bassoon and horn and the seal of beauty is set by a brief but telling cello solo. At length, the piano enters with an independent idea in light and rapid notes, while strings persist with their own thoughts. In the centre of the movement, however, piano takes over the strings' melody, transforming it into a lofty, noble statement. A solo horn contributes a few solemn comments now and at the end, as the pianist prepares for the finale.

One by one, other instruments join in until, with a virtuoso flourish, the piano gives way to the whole orchestra. Their frenzied troll dance is over in a flash as the piano gambols away with other new ideas. One of these is a quiet undulating theme, another is a decisive march. They accumulate tension and excitement, before coming to an emphatic climax, bringing welcome relief to the music.

At a slower tempo, a solo flute announces a new melody – one in which the triplet is once more prominent. This is music of misty fjords and birds soaring among the Norwegian peaks, and the orchestra and piano muse in a leisurely way until the scenery fades away.

In the distance, the beat of the Halling is heard again. The robust dance invades the music as before and takes us with a sense of inevitability to a climax and a vivid piano cadenza. Grieg then changes the rhythm (to 3/4), the tempo (to *Quasi presto*) and the key (to A major), for a featherlight dance that rapidly gains power for the thrilling finale: a full-blooded restatement of the flute's 'misty fjord' music.

Great interpreters

BBC Symphony Orchestra
The idea of a resident orchestra for broadcasting purposes was put forward at a very early stage of the British Broadcasting Corporation's life and, in 1924, some of the earliest such concerts were given at Central Hall Westminster by the 'Augmented Wireless Orchestra', whose conductors included Harty and Elgar. But it was only in 1930 that the BBC Symphony Orchestra was formed. With Sir Adrian Boult installed as conductor, it soon became a first-class orchestra. Its reputation spread throughout Europe and during the thirties, the world's most famous conductors guested with it. Included in this list were Strauss, Weingartner, Furtwängler and Walter. In 1935 it was the first British orchestra to be led by Toscanini.

The BBC Symphony continued to be the network's flagship – in the mid-1930's regional orchestras such as the Northern and Scottish were set up – and was led with increasing authority by Sir Adrian Boult. The company's retirement rules meant his departure in 1953, though he continued conducting elsewhere for almost 20 years. His successor, Sir Malcolm Sargent, maintained the high standards and, in later years, conductors have included Rudolf Kempe, Sir Colin Davis and Pierre Boulez. The orchestra still gives concerts at the Festival Hall each year and is still involved in the Proms. In the past two decades it has also toured in such diverse places as the USA, Japan, and the Warsaw Pact countries.

Stephen Bishop-Kovacevich (pianist)
Stephen Bishop was born of Yugoslav parents in Los Angeles in 1940 and he added the slavic patronym, Kovacevich, in 1975. He studied in Los Angeles with Lev Schorr from 1948 and made his first public appearance as a pianist in San Francisco in 1951. He continued his studies as well as making occasional appearances in the USA until, in 1959, he moved to London to study with Dame Myra Hess. His period with her proved fruitful and, in 1961, he made an extremely successful London debut at the Wigmore Hall. On the programme that night was Beethoven's *Diabelli Variations* and it is no coincidence that since then he has gone on to become one of the most sensitive and searching interpreters of Beethoven's piano works of his generation.

This success is partly due to his forceful style and partly to his unerring sense of form and structure. Although not an effortless virtuoso as, for example is Horowitz, Bishop-Kovacevich is an authoritative player with an ever-present emotional force behind his interpretations.

His pianistic abilities have long been recognized in Europe – in 1968 he gave the first performance of Richard Rodney Bennett's Piano Concerto, and in 1969 he delivered a complete Mozart Piano Concerto cycle in London, together with Geraint Jones. He has recorded extensively and has won awards for his playing of Bartók and Stravinsky.

FURTHER LISTENING

Holberg Suite, op.40
The Suite was first created as a piano suite written for the anniversary celebrations of the playwright Holberg, in 1884. Its pianistic origins still show through, but the version for string orchestra is much richer in nuance and expressive colour, and is justly more popular. The work contains much fine writing and ample evidence of Grieg's strong melodic inventiveness and sound musical thinking.

Lyric Pieces (for piano)
Ten books of these lyric miniatures were published during Grieg's lifetime. They fulfilled a purpose for both composer and amateur pianists throughout Europe who wanted small-scale works to play. Grieg thus benefitted from the royalties and also found an outlet for his Romantic impulse to capture fleeting moods and impressions in perfect miniature. It says a lot for these impulses and for the taste of those amateurs that the books have stood the test of time and are as fresh and charming today as they were a century ago.

Mountain Thrall, op.32
This short cantata is an unduly neglected product of Grieg's most fertile period. The words, taken from Old Norwegian verses and ballads, reflect a traditional interest in trolls and giants. Their stimulating effect on the composer's imagination results in a deeply moving musical accompaniment which follows every twist of the story and of the inner fears and dreams of the characters.

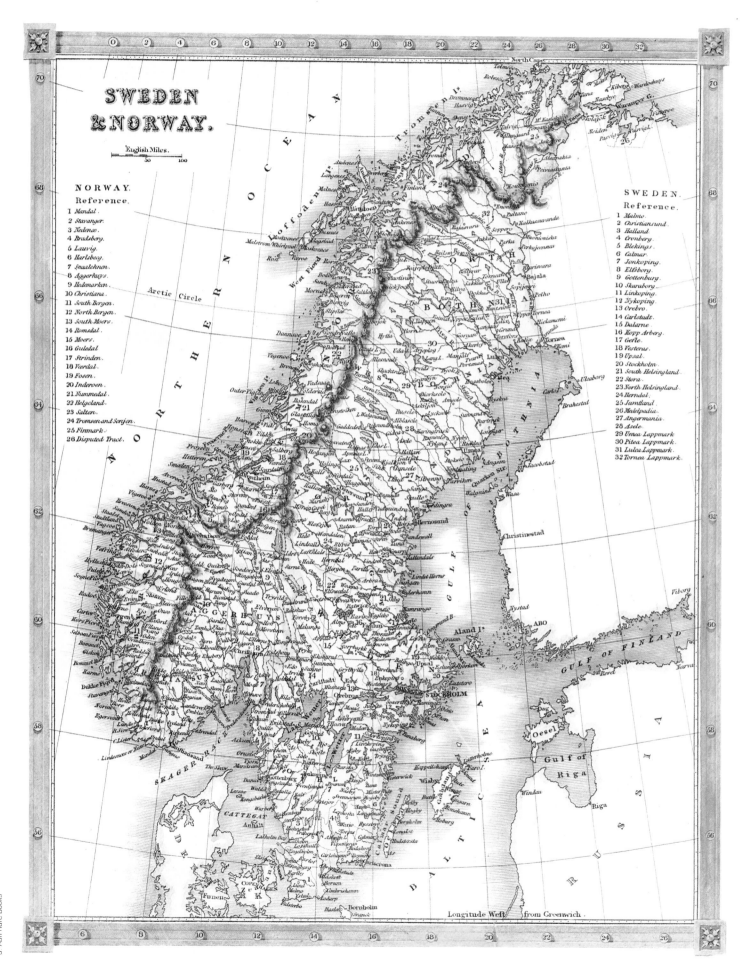

SWEDEN & NORWAY.

English Miles.
50   100

NORWAY.
Reference.

1 Mandal
2 Stavanger
3 Nedenœ
4 Bradsberg
5 Lauvig
6 Harlsberg
7 Smaalehnen
8 Aggerhuys
9 Hedemarken
10 Christiana
11 South Bergen
12 North Bergen
13 South Moers
14 Romsdal
15 Moers
16 Guledal
17 Strinden
18 Vardal
19 Fosen
20 Inderoen
21 Nummedal
22 Helgeland
23 Salten
24 Tromsen and Senjen
25 Finmark
26 Disputed Tract

SWEDEN.
Reference.

1 Malmœ
2 Christiansund
3 Halland
4 Crenberg
5 Blekings
6 Calmar
7 Jonkoping
8 Elfsborg
9 Gottenburg
10 Skaraborg
11 Linkoping
12 Nykoping
13 Orebro
14 Carlstadt
15 Dalarne
16 Kopp Arberg
17 Gefle
18 Vesterus
19 Upsal
20 Stockholm
21 South Helsingland
22 Stora
23 North Helsingland
24 Herrdal
25 Jamtland
26 Medelpadia
27 Angermania
28 Asele
29 Umea Lappmark
30 Piteä Lappmark
31 Lulea Lappmark
32 Tornea Lappmark

Longitude West from Greenwich.

IN THE BACKGROUND

'New Norway'

For over 500 years, Norway was ruled by foreign powers, first Denmark, then Sweden. But the 19th century saw Norway's national pride re-kindled as the country strove for, and won independence.

As the terror of the Viking years slowly faded from the memories of the people of Western Europe, so too did the glory of the kingdom of Norway and its kings of Bergen. Robbed of her trading riches by the power of the German Hanseatic League and decimated by the loss of almost two thirds of her already tiny population in the Black Death of 1349, Norway became almost a forgotten country quietly slipping into a subservient union with Denmark in 1380.

Over 400 years later, Norway was still so insignificant that it was again pushed into a similar union with Sweden. In the settlement of Europe following the defeat of Napoleon in 1814, Norway was simply 'given away' as a reward for the king of Sweden's loyalty to the great powers. Yet over the next 90 years, the people of Norway were gradually to find their courage again and, in the art of such figures as Edvard Grieg, their voice as well. By 1905, they were able to declare with conviction that they were a free and independent nation once more.

The story of Norway's struggle for nationhood runs parallel to the great nationalist movements that flamed all over Europe throughout the 19th century and, indeed, there are many similarities. There is the same deeply romantic strain in Norwegian nationalism, the same passionate love of the country's natural beauty and the same commitment to the country's folk heritage. Yet in Norway, the struggle was uniquely, and remarkably, bloodless. While elsewhere in Europe, nationalism was marked by noisy and violent episodes, the waves of Norwegian nationalism beat steadily against the bastions of foreign domination, slowly but surely eroding away all resistance.

Of course, there had been bloodshed in the past, indeed there were peasant rebellions as early as 1436, but such incidents became increasingly isolated as the Danes contrived to take the fire out of Norwegian protest by a series of judicious concessions. Such protest as there was became vocal rather than physical and Danish culture gradually swamped the small Norwegian population. Even the written word lost its power as Norway's written language was steadily replaced by Danish and by 1814 only a tiny proportion of the population even spoke Norse.

Nevertheless, the desire for independence never quite died out, and throughout the four centuries of Danish rule there was a steady undercurrent of nationalist feeling. Then, in the 18th century, demand for Norway's timber and mineral resources from England gave the country a period of increasing prosperity, and the population almost doubled. The buoyant economy and the rising number of Nor-

wegians gave the people a new awareness of their own identity. Consequently, pressure for concessions built up and a number of external events conspired to help the cause. First, in September 1807, Britain hijacked the Danish fleet to stop it being used by Napoleon, and then proceeded to blockade Denmark. The result was that Norway was cut off from the king in Copenhagen, and a separate administration had to be set up in Oslo, headed by Prince Christian Augustus. The second event was the Russian invasion of Swedish Finland in 1808-9. During the ensuing crisis in Sweden, Norwegian nationalists nominated Prince Christian Augustus heir to the Swedish throne – which would have effectively taken Norway from under Danish rule.

In the rising tide of anti-nationalism after the Napoleonic Wars Norway was ceded to the kingdom of Sweden (left) by Denmark in 1814. The Norwegian spirit and separate national identity was not so easily crushed however, and its ethnic and cultural traditions were maintained in everyday life (below).

In the latter half of the 19th century, women's rights took a leap forward. Spurred on by the writings of Camilla Collett (above) vast improvements were made to the law regarding inheritance and in the employment of women. There were great achievements, too, in the field of education and in 1882 the first female student was admitted to the University of Christiania (top).

The move away from rural cottage industries towards urbanization and industrialization (right) marked the turning point for Norwegian nationalism. Enthusiasm for the nationalist cause spread rapidly through the new industrial urban communities and independence, came within sight.

encouraged by Bernadotte, Norwegians were far from pleased. They made an immediate declaration of independence and established a representative national assembly at Eidsvoll to prepare their own constitution, based on American and French lines. The assembly defiantly adopted this constitution on May 17, 1814, and unanimously elected the Danish viceroy Christian Frederick as king of Norway.

Bernadotte reacted fiercely and sent in the Swedish troops, but negotiations started before there was any bloodshed. Norway contrived to keep the Eidsvoll constitution and its own legislative assembly, called the *Storting.* But despite this degree of progress the country was to remain under foreign domination — becoming part of a dual monarchy, presided over by the king of Sweden. Sweden held the power of veto over all the Storting's decisions, and Norway was to have no say whatsoever in foreign affairs. By this settlement the seeds of future conflict were clearly sown, for the Storting could pass legislation only to see it rejected out of hand by the Swedish king if he so chose. The Norwegians were in no position to object — the nationalist movement was not yet strong enough to resist.

However, one important concession for the Storting was wrung from the Swedes — namely that if three successive sessions in the Storting passed the same piece of legislation, the Swedish king lost his right of veto. The Norwegians immediately took advantage of this loophole and passed a bill abolishing its nobility in 1815. The Swedish king, of course, vetoed the bill. So they passed it again in 1818. Again the king vetoed it. In 1821, the Storting passed the bill for a third time, and Bernadotte, by then Charles XIV John, had, very reluctantly, to accept it as law. This tactic was to prove invaluable again in the future.

Unfortunately, Christian Augustus died suddenly in May 1810, leaving the Swedes open to a Danish claim to the throne. To prevent this, the Swedes adopted one of Napoleon's marshalls, Jean-Baptiste Bernadotte (later Charles XIV John), as heir to the throne, thereby hoping to neutralize any Danish ambitions.

The Storting
From this complex series of events, Norwegians gained nothing, but emerged with the conviction that it was no use looking to anyone else for help with their problems; they had to go it alone. So when the great powers awarded the sovereignty of Norway to Sweden under the Treaty of Kiel (January, 1814),

Working men identified very closely with the cause of nationalism, and it is no coincidence that the transition from individualism to mass democracy provided the final thrust towards achieving the goal of independence: a goal which undoubtedly diverted the minds of the workers (right) from the miseries of poor social conditions in the industrialized towns.

After 400 years of Danish rule, the Norwegians set about creating an independent native language – landsmål (language of the land) – which was based on rural dialects and Old Norse. Men such as Peter Christian Asbjørnsen (above) resurrected collections of Norwegian folk tales and introduced many native words and phrases into printed text.

Old Norway

The early years of the union with Sweden were far from easy for Norwegians. During the long years of the Napoleonic wars, their economy had suffered dreadfully because of the restrictions on trade. Poverty was widespread and, even in 1814, the population was still pitifully small, barely 900,000. Added to these problems was Bernadotte's increasingly high-handed approach to his Norwegian subjects. As far as he was concerned, Norway was Swedish property and the Treaty of Kiel the title deed for it. No wonder, then, that he should be so put out when Norwegians had the temerity to celebrate the 15th anniversary of their independence on 17 May 1829. Troops were sent in to disperse the celebrants but, fortunately, there was no bloodshed. Even so, many Norwegians continued to regard the 1814 constitution as a sign of their own independence and the existence of the Storting gave them a degree of self-respect that they had lacked for many years, a self-respect that could overcome many hardships.

In the years after the union with Sweden, the nationalist movement burgeoned among romantic intellectuals. Painters like J. C. Dahl explored the Norwegian landscape for their dramatic canvasses. Poets like Henrik Wergeland believed passionately in the potential for a genuinely Norwegian culture and way of life, and not only wrote about it but carried the idea into politics.

Just as in so many other countries at the time, Norwegians started to explore their own folk herit-

age and rediscover the culture that had seemed all but lost in the long years of Danish rule. In many ways, the very sparseness of the population had helped to preserve the distinctively Norwegian way of life in remote country districts. So when researchers from the towns went out to the outlying villages, they found a rich and lively tradition still flourishing. Peter Asbjørnsen and Jørgen Moe recorded many of the folk tales in their *Norske Folkeeventyr* (1841–4); M. Landstad and L. Lindemann did the same for folk songs. And musicians like Ole Bull, the violinist who encouraged the young Grieg to become a musician, tried to promote international acceptance of Norwegian folk music.

Most important of all, perhaps, was the attempt to redevelop a native Norwegian language to replace Danish, using the language of the country folk as a base. In 1836, the young Ivar Aasen formulated *Landsmål,* meaning 'language of the land', based on a synthesis of rural dialects and Old Norse from the Middle Ages. The publication of folk tales and poems which included many native elements of vocabulary and style gave the movement to promote the adoption of Landsmål an important fillip, and the movement continued to flourish throughout the century. Eventually, Landsmål was to take its place alongside Dano-Norwegian *(Riksmål).*

Norwegian artists continued to draw inspiration from the folk heritage of their country throughout the century. Many of the playwright Henrik Ibsen's early works, notably *Peer Gynt,* and the 'peasant

Educated as a lawyer, Johan Sverdrup (left) led the Venstre Party (a radical-liberal coalition) in the long fight against the government over the admission of ministers to the Storting (below). After the Venstre's victory he became the first Norwegian-elected prime minister within the newly empowered Storting. During his term of office (1884-1889) he introduced important reforms including trial by jury and the reorganization of the elementary school system.

Although under foreign rule for centuries, the spirit of Norway and the desire for independence lived on. The Norwegian people were passionately committed to the natural beauty of their land and to their own folk heritage (right).

tales' of the Bjørnstjerne Bjørnson, are based on the myths and legends of old Norway. And musicians, from Grieg's young friend Rikard Nordraak, who composed the Norwegian national anthem, *Ja, vi elsker,* to Johan Svendsen and, of course, Grieg himself, mined the same rich vein.

The growing nation

At first, the nationalist movement in Norway was immensely popular amongst romantic intellectuals, but had little broadly-based support. Between 1840 and 1860, however, Norway underwent rapid industrialization. Both the economy and the population grew. By 1850, Norway's population increased to 1½ million, almost double the figure for 1815. As the concentration of people in the towns accelerated, so mass support for the nationalist cause grew in strength. Men and women working close together began to appreciate their common problems and identities.

Equally important was the work of the Storting in spreading democracy by showing just what could be done if the people governed themselves. At first, power in the Storting was very much in the hands of the old ruling class. But after 1830 the assembly began to draw the peasantry into the political fold. A major victory was won in 1837 when, despite initial opposition from the Swedish king, the Storting placed local government in Norway on a popularly-elected base. And from the mid-1830s onwards a peasant party was represented in the Storting.

Peasant and liberal representation in the Storting rose steadily throughout the century, and with it rose the political consciousness of the people. During the 1840s and 1850s many liberal reforms in the fields of civil rights, religious tolerance and penal

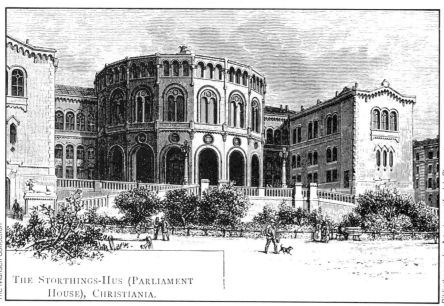

THE STORTHINGS-HUS (PARLIAMENT HOUSE), CHRISTIANIA.

reform were pushed through, despite the disapproval of the Swedish government, and Norwegians began to take great pride in their enlightenment. Norway pioneered many social reforms, including industrial accident compensation, and was well ahead of most European nations in extending the vote. Women's rights also took a step forward. An early campaigner for women's rights was Henrik Wergeland's sister, Camilla Collett, whose *The Country Governor's Daughter* highlighted the plight of middle class women forced into unhappy marriages by social pressure. The book was widely read, and had a great influence on Norwegian writers such as Ibsen and Jonas Lie. A great victory for women's rights was won in 1857 when women were given equal rights for inheritance and equal access to all forms of employment.

The rise of the Venstre

After 1870, the democratic base of the Storting continued to expand, and in the late 1870s, the city radical party, led by the great orator Johan Sverdrup, and the Peasant party united to form a broad left coalition (the Venstre) to push through further reforms. In particular, the Venstre wanted to move Norway towards full parliamentary government by bringing ministers, until then appointed by and responsible only to the Swedish king, under the control of the Storting. The Venstre brought in a bill to enforce ministers to attend sessions of the Venstre, and ensured that the bill was passed in three successive sessions, 1874, 1877 and 1880. But on the advice of the Conservative Prime Minister Stang, the king refused to accept the bill even the third time round.

After a sweeping victory in the 1882 elections,

Sverdrup and the Venstre felt strong enough to risk a showdown. Members of the cabinet were impeached for acting contrary to the wishes of the Storting. The king muttered vaguely about a coup d'état to bring the Norwegians into line, but he was restrained by Swedish Liberals. Sverdrup, then, took office as head of a Venstre ministry which clearly derived its authority from the Storting, and not the crown.

The final split

Now that internal freedom from Sweden had been achieved, an independent foreign policy, and thereby complete independence, became the goal. Norway's prosperity depended increasingly on her large merchant navy and Norwegians began to demand their own consular service to protect these trading interests. Then, in the general elections of 1891, the Venstre won an impressive majority on the issue of a separate foreign and consular service for Norway.

To make their intentions clear on the issue,

In the late 19th century anti-monarchical dramas, satires and cartoons (left) fuelled the republican as well as the nationalist cause. However, the republican cause never really became a strong force because of Norway's long-standing royalist traditions.

King Oscar (below), seated with members of the Swedish Royal family, was persuaded by Swedish liberals not to take repressive measures against Norway, which was then under Swedish control.

Mary Evans Picture Library

*The ministry (left)
whose resignation
precipitated the final
split with Sweden.
Under new legislation
King Oscar was unable
to appoint another
cabinet and as a result
received a
proclamation of
independence from
Norway – and notice of
his own deposition.*

Norway abandoned the emblem of the Union from her merchant flag and began to build forts along the border with Sweden. When King Oscar refused to accept their bill establishing a Norwegian consular service, the entire Norwegian ministry resigned. Of course, the king was unable to appoint an alternative cabinet with the support of the Storting. So the Storting resolved that the monarchy had ceased to function. A proclamation to Oscar was prepared which ran:

The Storting authorises the members of the resigned ministry to continue as the Norwegian government . . . and to administer the authority granted to the King . . . The union with Sweden is dissolved in consequence of the King's ceasing to function as the King of Norway.

Members of the Storting voted unanimously for the resolution. The Prime Minister Christian Michelsen closed his address to the Storting in the early hours of 7 June 1905 with the words, 'God preserve our fatherland.' Crowds were ecstatic, and accompanied many of the Government leaders to their homes, drinking toasts to the 'New Norway'.

During the summer of 1905, the situation was tense with both sides mobilizing their armed forces. But an amicable agreement was soon reached. Sweden sensibly agreed to let Norway separate, and confirmed this by providing a 25-mile neutral border zone, which still exists today. Norway, as a conciliatory gesture, offered to accept a Swedish prince as head of the Norwegian monarchy and agreed to Swedish requests for a referendum on the issue of independence. The true force of Norwegian nationalism was revealed when a vote of 368,208 in favour of independence was recorded. Only 184 voted against.

There was some talk of a republic, as there had been for some years, but the traditions of Norway's former greatness were closely associated with the rise of monarchy, from the days of Olav the Saint, and a second referendum indicated a 4 to 1 majority in favour of a monarchy.

The aged King Oscar II of Sweden felt too deeply irritated to accept the Norwegian suggestion of a Swedish nomination. The Norwegians eventually accepted King Edward VII of England's nomination, his Danish son-in-law, who became King Haakon VII. Most important in Norwegian eyes was Haakon's two-year-old son, who would grow up in Norway and learn the history, traditions and language of his adopted country.

Mary Evans Picture Library

Having decided that a monarchy was the best guarantee of stability in a small state, the Norwegians were faced with the question of who should be king. In the absence of a Swedish nomination, they finally chose King Edward VII of England's Danish son-in-law, who later became Haakon VII. The new king with his queen, Maud, is shown left, receiving a peasant delegation in Christiania.

THE GREAT COMPOSERS

Jean Sibelius

1865–1957

Jean Sibelius lived in a country with a precarious national identity, but his stirring compositions helped to unite and celebrate the Finland he loved. Although in later years, he turned to a more classical style, his orchestral works based on Finnish legends were remarkably personal and expressive. In his symphonic works, Sibelius first presents fragments of his themes, building them to completion in the middle sections, then dissolving them again in a modern style that was to influence later composers profoundly. In his Symphony no. 2 and Finlandia, analysed in the Listener's Guide, this quite individual approach is apparent, as is his love of his Finnish homeland. In the face of attempts by Russia to dominate Finland, its people clung increasingly to the vestiges of their national heritage as In The Background describes; the music of Sibelius was a proud part of this heritage.

Jean Sibelius studied law in Helsinki before turning to his greater passion, music. He continued his musical training in Berlin and Vienna, but it was not until his return to Finland in 1891 that his musical ideas took shape when he decided to capture the growing spirit of nationalism in his music. By the late 1890s he was held in such high esteem in Finland that the government awarded him a lifetime pension. His international reputation grew, and the early years of the century saw great personal triumphs for Sibelius, with successful tours of England and the United States. Yet, he remained a deeply self-critical man, sometimes so unsatisfied by some of his work that he forbade its performance. Perhaps this self-doubt contributed to his early retirement in the late 1920s. His popularity throughout the world continued to grow, but Sibelius himself lived quietly in his country home until his death in 1957.

'Finland awakes'

His imagination fired by the haunting beauty of his country and its past, Sibelius wrote music which not only won him acclaim abroad but also embodied the spirit of Finnish nationalism.

Jean Sibelius was born in Finland on 8 December 1865. At that time, Finland, under Russian rule, although supposedly autonomous, was a country with a precarious national identity. Swedish was the official language and the Finnish-speaking members of the population were regarded as second-class citizens.

His parents – Christian and Maria Sibelius – lived in the small garrison town of Hämeenlinna in south-central Finland. His father – a military doctor – died in a cholera epidemic when Jean was only two years old, and the three Sibelius children were brought up by their mother in the home of their maternal grandmother and spinster aunt. Summers were spent at the home of his other grandmother in Loviisa. He also paid regular visits to one of his uncles, Pehr, an eccentric bachelor with strong interests in music and astronomy who lived in the coastal town of Turku, but otherwise the influences on him during his early years were overwhelmingly female.

His ancestry was part Swedish and part Finnish,

Jean Sibelius (right), Finland's first internationally acclaimed composer, drew much of the inspiration for his music from his deep love of the countryside where he grew up (below).

Sibeliusmuseum, Åbo, Finland

Werner Holmberg 'Hop Gardens in Hame'. Art Museum of the Ateneum, Finland

but as members of the middle class the family was Swedish-speaking. Jean was taught some Finnish from the age of eight to prepare him for entry to the local grammar school, which was exceptional in being one of the few schools in the country where lessons were taught in Finnish. He had a small number of close friends but does not seem to have been naturally gregarious and had little liking for team sports and other group activities. He also found many of his lessons boring; he dreamed a lot of his time away and was really only stimulated by mathematics and natural history.

This close identification with nature remained with him to the end of his life and was the single most profound influence on his music. Above the published score of his last major composition, the tone-poem *Tapiola*, he wrote these lines:

Widespread they stand, the Northland's dusky forests,
Ancient, mysterious, brooding savage dreams;
And within them dwells the Forest's mighty God
And wood-sprites in the gloom weave magic secrets.

Sibelius's background ensured that he came into contact with music at an early age; families made their own entertainments, and it was the rule rather than the exception for children to learn to sing and play a musical instrument. Jean enjoyed listening to music and even composed a little piece for violin and cello called *Water Drops* at the age of ten, but this was not considered exceptional, though it shows

Sibelius was the second child of Christian and Maria Sibelius (above). From an early age his imagination was fired by the vast and overwhelming grandeur of his homeland (below).

that he was keen to create his own music. It was only when he was presented with a violin at the age of 14 that he developed real enthusiasm; he took lessons with the local bandmaster and for the next ten years his ambitions were centred on becoming a virtuoso player. He also developed a more serious interest in musical form, especially after his discovery and study of Marx's *Kompositionslehre*. However, music-making was not really approved by the family as a profession so when he left the Grammar School in 1885 it was to study law at Helsinki University. He also enrolled at the Academy of Music as a special student to study violin and composition under the director, Martin Wegelius. It was soon clear that the legal studies were taking a back seat; he was visited one day by an uncle who noticed his text book lying open on the window-sill, its pages yellowed by months of exposure to the sun. Perceptively he advised Sibelius to take up music full-time.

A full-time music student

He acquitted himself well at the Academy of Music, although by the time he was due to leave he had probably concluded that he would never be a violinist of the top rank – he had after all made a fairly late start. He had received a lot of encouragement from Wegelius in composition and in his final term produced a String Trio in A Major and a String Quartet in A minor.

Perhaps more important than all the academic training he received at this time were the people with whom he came in contact. In 1888 Wegelius had engaged the brilliant young German–Italian Ferruccio Busoni as a piano teacher. Busoni was about the same age as Sibelius and in spite of

Sibeliusmuseum, Åbo, Finland

differences in background and experience – Busoni had been hailed as a prodigy from early childhood – the two had an immediate rapport. Although he was basically shy, Sibelius would open out in the company of trusted friends and express his great capacity for enjoying food, wine and conversation. Many long evenings in Helsinki were spent at a favourite restaurant, Kämps, in the company of Busoni and two other friends, Adolf Paul and Armas Järnefelt (later his brother-in-law).

Adolf Paul had enrolled at the Helsinki Music Academy at the same time as Sibelius to study piano, and in the autumn of 1889 both young men went to Berlin to continue their studies. Paul soon decided that his main talents were literary rather than musical, and set about writing an autobiographical novel entitled 'A Book about a Man'. It contained a character called Sillen. Mercurial, passionate, extravagant, but with his energies still largely unfocussed, this is Sibelius in thin disguise.

Frequently indulging his natural generosity and taste for high living, after two months in Berlin Sibelius had exhausted his state grant and had to appeal for help from home. He had studied con-scientiously enough under Albert Becker, but the teaching was unimaginative and he found little encouragement for his own individual talent. But all was not wasted – Berlin did offer him the opportunity to hear much more music. He attended the world premiere of Strauss's *Don Juan,* Bülow's performances of the Beethoven piano sonatas, and recitals by the Joachim Quartet.

Importantly for his own development as a nationalist composer he made the acquaintance in Berlin of Robert Kajanus. Kajanus was founder and

director of the Helsinki Philharmonic Orchestra, but because of the extraordinary feud between the Music Academy and the orchestra Sibelius had not met him earlier – Wegelius even forbade his students to attend their concerts. Kajanus was in Berlin to conduct his *Aino* Symphony – a tone-poem for chorus and orchestra based on legends from the Finnish national epic, the *Kalevala.* What Sibelius thought of the symphony we do not know, but the possibilities of the Kalevala as a source of musical inspiration were awakened in him.

In 1890 on his return to Finland, Sibelius spent much of the summer with his friend from the Academy, Armas Järnefelt, and his family. Armas came from a very distinguished background – his father, General August Järnefelt, was a famous soldier and government administrator and his mother was an aristocrat with a great interest in the arts. He had two brothers, Arvid and Eero, who were to become a writer and a painter respectively, and a younger sister, Aino. Still only eighteen, she fell for Sibelius at first sight and by the end of the summer they had become secretly engaged.

In the autumn Sibelius went to Vienna to continue his studies. He had a letter of introduction written by Busoni to Brahms, who, in his customary way, refused to meet him – but they did meet by accident in a cafe though nothing more came of this. Instead, Sibelius studied under two other leading Viennese musical figures, Karl Goldmark and Robert Fuchs. In 1891, his studies over, he returned to Finland and spent the summer in the family house at Loviisa.

Suddenly, during the space of a few months, every-thing seemed to work towards the realization of his ambitions. The visits to Berlin and Vienna may have

At the age of 20 Sibelius left Hämeenlinna and went to the bustling capital city of Helsinki (above) to study law – his family felt that a musical career was not respectable. However, he also enrolled as a part-time student at the Academy of Music. After only two terms he gave up his law studies to pursue his own cherished ambition to become a full-time music student.

Considering his late start in serious musical studies he acquitted himself well at the Academy. For his final term he composed a String Trio in A Major *and a* String Quartet in A Minor, *accompanying the latter with an atmospheric pencil sketch (above).*

As a student Sibelius, together with his Academy friends, frequented the many cafés of Helsinki, including Kämps Hotel (below). Although not active in Helsinki society he did come into contact with many members of Finnish cultural life. In Berlin (bottom), however, he indulged his taste for high living.

been valuable experiences in some respects, but creatively had offered him little. Back amongst the scenery he loved so much, and surrounded by family and friends, he relaxed and his musical plans took shape. But external events were to provide the prompt and inspiration for his work.

At this time, Russia was beginning to exert further control over Finland's already limited independence. In response, particularly among the young, a growing feeling of nationalism began to percolate through the country – a reaction against being swamped and lumped in with the sprawling giant of Russia. Sensing the mood and wanting to contribute to expressing Finland's identity, the idea of using legends from the Kalevala came back to him, and he

set to work with a new urgency.

By the spring of 1892 Sibelius had completed a massive five-movement tone-poem for soloists, chorus and orchestra which he called *Kullervo*. It was given its first performance by the Helsinki Philharmonic on April 29, 1892, with Sibelius himself conducting. He had at last found his own voice, and it brought him instant acclaim, yet, in a pattern to be repeated many times with other works, he was not satisfied with his composition and after a few performances he withdrew it for revision – indeed, he never allowed it to be performed again in his lifetime.

One effect of success was to pave the way for his marriage to Aino Järnefelt, which took place in June the same year. After a honeymoon in the Eastern province of Karelia, the couple went to Helsinki where Sibelius took up teaching posts at the Musical Academy and at Kajanus' Orchestral School.

During the next seven years, a number of orchestral compositions appeared, mostly inspired by Finnish legend – *En Saga,* the *Karelia Suite,* the *Lemminkäinen Suites* and finally, in 1899, *Finlandia.*

Under the so-called February Manifesto of 1899, the Russians virtually crushed Finnish independence by severely restricting the right of assembly and freedom of speech. A theatrical pageant was staged in Helsinki in November with a strong patriotic theme, and *Finlandia* was composed to accompany the final tableau, entitled 'Finland Awakes'. It immediately acquired the status of a second national anthem and has remained the composer's most famous piece. Much more significant though, in terms of his work and establishment of a personal musical language, was the appearance in the same year of the First Symphony.

Although firmly established as his country's leading composer, Sibelius still did not feel financially secure. He was by now in receipt of a state pension, awarded to him in 1897 as compensation for his

National Museum of Finland, Helsinki

lph von Menzel 'The Supper Ball'. Archiv für Kunst und Geschichte

National Museum of Finland

In 1888 Sibelius and the brilliant young German–Italian musician Ferruccio Busoni (above and right) became firm friends. Busoni, one of the first to realize and appreciate Sibelius's talent, was always an enthusiastic champion of Sibelius's international reputation.

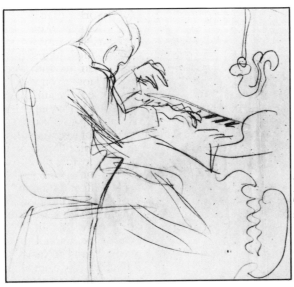

On his return from Berlin, Sibelius met and became engaged to Aino Järnefelt (far left) in 1890. Later, her brother, the painter, Eero Järnefelt, drew him at the piano.

failure to win the post of Professor of Composition at Helsinki University – the job went instead to Kajanus. The pension guaranteed him a basic minimum income and the gesture showed the esteem in which he was already held by his countrymen. His teaching also provided him with a steady income and although he was a somewhat unorthodox teacher his pupils rememberd him with warm affection. He also had very little business sense, accepting modest lump-sum payments for some of his compositions when a royalty arrangement would have made him a small fortune. However, matters improved somewhat after his introduction to the German publishing firm of Breitkopf and Härtel.

International reputation

Baron Axel Carpelan, together with Kajanus, organized a European tour by the Helsinki Philharmonic in 1900 which triumphantly introduced Sibelius' music to audiences outside Finland. Carpelan put 5000 marks towards the cost of a trip to Italy at his disposal. This meant that he could take time off from teaching to compose and during this extended holiday with his family in the spring of 1901 begin work on the Second Symphony. Later that year he was asked to conduct two of the *Lemminkäinen Legends* at the Heidelberg Festival. The Second Symphony had its premiere in March 1902 in Helsinki, and soon afterwards he was turning his thoughts to a violin concerto.

But although these were quite prolific years, Sibelius was in fact growing restless and discontented. Finding the city of Helsinki a disagreeable place for composition, he turned more and more inward in his search for inspiration. In the spring of 1904 he purchased some property on a wooded hillside just outside the village of Järvenpää, about 35 kilometers north east of Helsinki, and had a large traditional-style villa built there.

Although Järvenpää, which was his home for the rest of his life, provided the peaceful atmosphere he needed, he was by no means cut off from life outside. Helsinki was less than an hour away by train and he continued to visit his favourite restaurants and hotels and also to travel abroad when he could afford it. Between 1905 and 1908 he made several trips to England and said that he was so well entertained that he 'did not become acquainted with English coins'. In 1908 on the second of these trips he conducted his Third Symphony, which had been premiered in Helsinki the previous year.

During this time Sibelius' was troubled by pains in the throat, and a tumour was diagnosed. After an initial examination in Helsinki, he travelled to Berlin for specialist treatment and after several operations a malignant tumour was successfully removed. The threat of recurrence remained and he was forbidden alcohol and cigars. The experience made him acutely aware of his own mortality and the music he composed over the next few years, especially the String Quartet *Voces intimae* and the Fourth Symphony, reflect this in their meditative mood.

Sibelius in America

In 1914 Sibelius made a trip to the United States at the invitation of a millionaire music-lover, Carl Stoeckel. Stoeckel had built a concert hall in the

Firenze,
Case di S Jacopo sull'Arno.

Sibelius's international reputation began to take wing after a tour undertaken by the Helsinki Philharmonic Orchestra under Kajanus in 1900. They visited Stockholm, Lübeck, Hamburg and Paris, where the concerts they gave were part of the Finnish contribution to the Paris Exhibition (centre). In 1901, one of the patrons of the tour, Baron Axel Carpelan, a close friend of Sibelius, arranged for sufficient funds to be put at his disposal so that he could take a year off from teaching to spend time composing. He went with his family to Italy where he worked on the Second Symphony. On his return journey he visited Florence (above) where he considered the idea of setting part of Dante's Divine Comedy *to music.*

grounds of his estate at Norfolk, Connecticut, and every summer, in association with the Litchfield County Choral Union, he held a music festival there. The festival has been described as 'America's Bayreuth' but it lacked the latter's almost religious atmosphere. Sibelius composed and conducted a new tone-poem, *The Oceanides*. He was treated with great warmth and generosity, and after the festival was over he and Stoeckel travelled to a number of places of interest, including Niagara Falls, in Stoeckel's luxurious motor car or private Pullman coach. Sibelius's sole regret seems to have been that he was still too nervous about his throat condition to accept the fine wines and cigars which his host pressed upon him. Before he returned home he was presented with a Doctorate of Music from Yale.

Shortly after he came back, World War I broke out in Europe. Sibelius was depressed by the appalling news of the slaughter and there was the added irritation that communication with his German publishers became very difficult. Nonetheless, 1915 was a year of great celebration – his 50th birthday – and he marked it by conducting the premiere of his Fifth Symphony. The day was declared a national holiday and he was showered with gifts and tributes from all over the world. This symphony seems to have had particularly happy associations for him; he once said that his only memory of his father was of sitting on his knee and being shown a picture of a swan, and as he was completing the score of this symphony he was delighted to see a flock of swans rise from the lake and circle the house three times before flying away.

1918 was a hard year for Sibelius, and indeed for all his countrymen. Following the Russian Revolution of 1917, a bitter class struggle developed in Finland and both sides were soon taking up arms. In January 1918 the existing government declared the country

independent of Russia, but was overthrown in a left-wing coup a month later. Away from the capital, there were many violent incidents and Sibelius' own life was considered to be in danger, especially in view of the patriotic music he had written. His house was twice searched by soldiers. Eventually, he was persuaded to leave the countryside and take his wife and children to Helsinki to stay with his brother, who was a doctor at one of the city hospitals. Fortunately, by the summer hostilities had come to an end, an independent government had been restored and the family was able to return to Ainola.

Retirement and silence

The next few years saw the publication of his last two symphonies and he again went on travels abroad. But the appearance of a tone-poem *Tapiola* in 1926 effectively marked the end of his creative life. The publication of this work coincided with his retirement as a conductor. The thirty years which followed, for Sibelius lived to a great old age, have become known as The Silence from Järvenpää.

The reasons for his retirement were many: his instincts lay in more traditionally rooted music than that coming from more avant-garde composers like Schoenberg and Stravinsky. On a personal level he deeply felt the loss of his friend Axel Carpelan who had died, and his drinking had become a problem. It proved difficult for him to regain the position he had held in pre-war Europe. Sibelius did not leave Finland during the 1930s and so never felt at first hand the esteem in which he was held in Britain and

Following the Russian Revolution of 1917 and the bitter class struggle in Finland, in January 1918 the existing government declared Finland, represented in the political cartoon (above left) as an elk harried by the Russian wolf pack, free from intimidation and dominance by Russia. A left-wing coup ensued and during the bitter fighting in the countryside, Sibelius and his wife (above) were advised to take refuge in Helsinki. Later that year they returned to their beloved home, Ainola.

America.

Life in retirement was hardly quiet though, as Sibelius' five surviving daughters had all married and produced children, and there was an army of grandchildren and great-grandchildren for whom he expressed interest and concern. Finally, there was the vexed question of the Eighth Symphony.

Whether this work ever existed is not known, but many musicians and journalists seemed to think that it ought to, and kept pestering Sibelius for information about it. He became adept at parrying these requests, remarking that to publish and to compose were two quite different things, but it seems likely that if there was a score, it did not meet his own exacting demands and was subsequently destroyed. The loss of creative ability caused him worry, even guilt, as he sometimes felt he was not justifying his generous state pension.

On September 20, 1957, Malcolm Sargent was conducting a performance of the Fifth Symphony in Helsinki. Normally, at least some members of Sibelius' immediate family would have been there, but that afternoon he had suffered a stroke and at a quarter to nine in the evening, he died. Two days earlier, watching the migrating cranes pass over his home, he had had a premonition of death. His body lay in state in Helsinki Cathedral before he was finally laid to rest at Järvenpää, in the grounds of his beloved Ainola.

Orchestral works

Sibelius's Symphony no. 2 and Finlandia are powerful expressions of Finnish national spirit – revealing both a deep love of his homeland and his mastery of orchestral colour and form.

Symphony no. 2 in D major, op. 43

The appeal of Sibelius's mighty Second Symphony can only be properly understood when seen against the background of nationalism that was emerging in Finland at the time of its composition. After centuries of foreign domination, first by Sweden, then by Russia, a national renaissance was under way when Sibelius was born in 1865. This climate was to have a profound effect on the boy who was to become Finland's leading composer.

Upsurge of Nationalism

The Finns were trying to restore their sense of national identity by rediscovering their own mythology and literature, and by resurrecting their own language; Swedish was still the official language of the civil service. Sibelius's first major work, *Kullervo,* a massive five-movement piece for chorus and orchestra based on the national epic *Kalevala,* was an enormous success when it was first performed in April 1892. His interest in national and patriotic issues was further heightened by his marriage to Aino Järnefelt, whose father was a provincial Governor and an ardent supporter of the efforts to restore the Finnish language to official usage.

After Sibelius had completed his First Symphony in 1898, a series of repressive measures was introduced by the Tsarist régime, causing another upsurge of nationalist feeling. The February Manifesto of the following year set out to restrict still further the freedom and already very limited political representation granted to the Finns. Sibelius reacted by pouring out a spate of nationalist works, including a series of tableaux written for the November celebrations in aid of the Press Pension Fund, a seemingly innocuous enough event, which however became a platform for a political demonstration. The last of these tableaux was called *Finland Awakes,* and retitled *Finlandia* when he revised it the following year.

Sibelius was now a national figure, and in the following years he was to become an international one. When his own works received an enthusiastic reception in the foreign countries he toured with the Finnish Orchestra under his friend Kajanus, his thoughts turned to a new symphony. His friends were urging him to

This portrait of a group of artists and intellectuals (left), shows a bleary-eyed Sibelius (near right), and, seated next to him – also rather the worse for wear – Robert Kajanus. Kajanus, a gifted composer and conductor, was to be the greatest interpreter of Sibelius's music.

spend an autumn in Italy and devote himself to composition. Carpelan, one of his most loyal friends managed to raise the money to finance the trip, but it was not until February that Sibelius arrived in Rapallo. There he laboured with a work he called *Festival,* based on the story of Don Juan; the main theme of the Andante of the Second Symphony still owes something to this original concept. He returned to Finland via Florence, where he toyed with the idea of setting part of Dante's *Divine Comedy* to music, and this digression delayed the completion of the symphony. When it finally got its first performance in January 1902, its immediate appeal to the patriotic fervour of the time made it an instant success.

A new musical voice

The symphony establishes from its very first bars a new, quite individual, musical voice, and it is difficult to realize that it was written by a man to whom the music of Dvořák, Tchaikovsky, and Brahms was 'contemporary'. Sibelius's personal signature is immediately apparent in the symphony's orchestral colour and architectural form. Typical elements of his orchestral language are the cross-hatching of the strings, the powerfully expressive writing for the violins (recalling the fact that for many years Sibelius wanted to be a virtuoso violinist rather than a composer), the long sustained brass chords building to a slow crescendo, the long *pedal points* (bass notes held over a passage which includes clashes of harmony), and the openness of the textures.

In structural terms too, an entirely new principle is apparent, although it was foreshadowed in Beethoven's last quartets – the principle of 'condensation': Mahler, speaking of his own Seventh Symphony, described this as 'a profound logic that creates an inner connection between all the motifs'. Instead of adopting the classical format of introducing complete themes and then breaking them down to analyze them in a new light in a development section, Sibelius starts with the fragments, wisps, scraps, and hints of themes. These are built up into an organic whole only in the middle section of the movement, and then dissolved back into their original particles at the very end. This approach is truly modern. It belongs to the nuclear age, just as Mahler's symphonies belong to the Freudian era. The laws that operate in Sibelius's symphonies are the laws of physics; particles of matter swirl until they are caught by a nucleus, resulting in a tremendous release of energy.

Feeling its way through vaporous mists, Sibelius's Second Symphony unfolds to reveal a vast primeval landscape (left). There is a tremendous sense of latent energy, as croaking bassoons and rustling strings conjure up the first stirrings of the forces of nature. Seen within its contemporary context, the music seems to express the powerful awakening of Finnish nationalist feeling.

Between autumn 1901 and spring 1902, Sibelius stayed in the coastal resort of Rapallo (right). There, walking in the surrounding hills 'covered with pines, olive trees and cypresses', he found the inspiration to write the Second Symphony.

Sibelius starts with the inorganic, with the granite rocks of his homeland: 'when we see those granite rocks', he said to a friend, 'we know why we are able to treat the orchestra as we do.'

Then, building from the inorganic, he manages to catch the sound of the wind in the forests, the 'pedal notes' of elemental forces working on nature. No other composer has conjured up so powerfully the Earth before Man. As Sir Neville Cardus wrote:

The music of Sibelius is as though the sights and sounds of his country, the air, and light, and darkness, the legends and the history, had by some inner generative force become audible in terms of rustling violins; horn-calls out of a void, brass that swells to us in short gusts like music blown on a wind, beginning and ending almost as soon as heard; oboes and flutes that emit the clucking of weird fowl; bassoons that croak in the swamps and mists . . . In Sibelius, the forces of nature seem to live, move and have being of their own.

Programme notes

The Second Symphony is scored for 2 flutes, 2 oboes, 2 clarinets, 2 bassoons, 4 horns, 3 trumpets, 3 trombones, tuba, kettle-drums, and the traditional string choir.

First movement: Allegretto – Poco allegro – Tranquillo, ma poco a poco ravvivando il tempo al allegro

The strings open with hushed, repeated chords, giving a sense of inert passivity. Over them, the oboes and clarinets state the first theme, a melody of transparent simplicity (typical of Sibelius), which is then repeated three times.

Example 1

It is punctuated by a horn motive, acting as a pendant and link, which is later to play an important role; this little figure is a compressed tune in itself, and is a fine example of Sibelius's orchestral crafts-manship in the way he has dovetailed it so neatly into the woodwind texture. Then there is a pause. Flutes sound forlornly, answered by bassoons. But then the drums roll, and the bassoon figure climbs to a crescendo. The flutes shrill for all their worth, and the violins make a rhetorical statement, like a rather hammy actor

Hans F. Gude 'Mountain Region' Nasjonalgalleriet, Oslo. Photo Jacques Lathion

The second movement, with its open textures and granite-like solidity of structure, evokes the rugged landscape of Scandinavia (above).

declaiming with his hand on his heart, yet nevertheless displaying his art, as Sibelius here displays his knowledge and love of the emotional range of the violin's language.

After some discussion by the woodwind, the tempo changes, and the strings start a pizzicato figure which builds up to the most important of the second group of themes.

Example 2

This melody is, in fact, a long sustained pedal note of pent up feeling, which ends

Understanding music: national anthems

Television has made us all familiar with the scene: long shot of Olympic medallists in triumphant pyramid; close up of the champion as the first gutsy chords of the national anthem strike up; cut to the country's flag as it shakily climbs its pole; back to the champion to focus on the tearful mixture of pride, patriotism and un-adulterated joy. No matter how dull and directionless the anthem may be – they sometimes sound as though some mischief-maker has wantonly shuffled the score sheets – we voyeurs from afar are caught up in the magic of the moment.

God Save the Queen no longer has British cinema audiences rising un-certainly from their seats, but at international soccer matches it is sung out with furious gusto.

The original intention of the anthem was to pay homage to the Sovereign, and this is still the case on those grand ceremonial occasions. The hymn-like and stately *God Save the King/Queen* is the oldest of them all. It first became popular during the Jacobite rising: Thomas Arne's ver-sion was sung defiantly in 1745 by the Theatre Royal's audience in Drury Lane following the defeat of John Cope's army at Prestonpans by Bon-nie Prince Charlie.

At one time, like a pair of baggy trousers, *God Save the King/Queen* fitted all who tried it on. Denmark, Switzerland, Russia, the USA, Liech-tenstein – all found it comfortable. Canada, with a few Gallic complaints, still has to, though Australia since 1974 has had its very own – *Advance Australia Fair*. A well-known patriotic song, it was chosen after a

Museo Storico, Strasburg. Photo Mauro Pucciarelli

La Marseillaise, the French anthem, was written as a marching song for Marshal Lukner's army of the Rhine in 1792 by Claude-Joseph Rouget de Lisle (above).

competition with 1200 entries failed to produce anything as acceptable.

It's hard to believe that Russians once sang *God Save the Tsar* to the music of the British anthem. Pre-dictably it was not favoured by the Bolsheviks who, in 1917, replaced it with the *Internationale* which had a text written by a Parisian transport worker during the siege of 1871. The present anthem, written as a party song for the Bolsheviks during World War II, begins 'Unbreakable union of freeborn republic'. The *Internationale* is still sung in rousing fashion by left-wing groups in certain countries.

Patriotic fervour can be highly inspirational: *La marseillaise* France's national anthem, was written in a single night in 1792 by Claude-Joseph Rouget de Lisle. Written originally as a marching song for the army of the Rhine, it achieved heart-pounding popularity (and its new name) when it was sung by a battalion of volunteers from Marseilles as they entered Paris in July 1792. The Second Empire's attempt to replace it with something a little less 'revolutionary' failed – the stirring anthem marches on.

Inspiration for Francis Scott Key took the form of the American flag flying defiantly over Fort McHenry in 1814. He was being detained at the time on board an English frigate, part of a fleet that had been bombarding Fort McHenry. He sat down and wrote *The Star-spangled Banner* to music that had been written, ironically by an English composer.

The texts

The words are rarely masterpieces of lyricism. Some dwell on the beauty of the land – Austria's anthem, written allegedly by members of Mozart's masonic lodge, begins: 'Land of mountains, land of streams'. Others are unashamedly jingoistic in tone – Egypt's 'O, my weapon, How I long to clutch thee!' is positively ghoulish, while 'Mexicans, at the call of war take your swords and bridles' is plainly bellicose, and the Senegalese summons for everyone to '. . . pluck the koras and strike the balafos, the red lion has roared', is mystifyingly evocative. Some texts are quite specific, like Chad's 'People of Chad, arise and get to work', and some encyclopedic: 'Khmers are known throughout the world as the descendants of a nation of glorious warriors', from Kampuchea. Perhaps most eloquent are those with no words!

at the onrushing strings, and a threatening underswell on the cellos breaks through to the surface, reinforced by the bassoons, like a volcanic eruption of pent up lava. As the storm subsides, a most sinister passage follows, where single drum beats stake out a hostile no-man's land while lonely clarinets flutter above. Then the strings take over this figure, mixing it with their own rhetorical melody to build a colossal climax, and steer the movement to a brass blaze of triumph.

The little horn pendant now returns to lead to the restatement, and the movement ends as it began, with the inevitable logic

The stirring finale is a work of full-blooded patriotism, with a direct appeal to the emotions. Its heroic character is reflected in Altdorfer's chaotic battle scene (below), where bright pennants float above the heads of a sea of horses and warriors.

Tres Riches Heures du duc de Berry. Musee Conde. Chantilly/Photo Giraudon

Following the brilliantly orchestrated third movement, comes the sweeping melody of the finale, punctuated by brass fanfares (above). This heraldic device enhances the nationalist flavour, creating a mood of splendid pageantry.

with a plunging interval of a fifth. The strings now really get worked up, with drums rolling, aided by flutes and bassoons breaking through to punctuate, and almost syncopate, the rhythm. A climax builds up, with the woodwind repeating the theme, and suddenly we are plunged back into the opening theme, which has now become a tailpiece to this second melody. 'In my end is my beginning' — what a marvellous thematic unity is here achieved by Sibelius.

The strings hush, and the development of the main theme now begins on the oboe, which somehow seems to compress it, with the bassoons darkly answering. Now we are in a twilight world. Woodwind stab

of a natural force that has expended its energy. Sibelius has shown us a vast landscape, and the energy that went into its making.

Second movement: Tempo andante, ma rubato – Andante sostenuto

A mysterious drum roll sets off a rather puzzled theme on the double basses, which plod somewhat hopelessly about in boots of pizzicato quavers. When the cellos join in the theme sounds a little more hopeful. Then, over softly rolling drums, the bassoons enter with a most mournful melody, marked *lugubre* (lugubrious) in the score. Clarinets and oboes join in, providing a wonderful span of colour and space, as they play over the double basses, punctuated by throbs on the horns and drums. A deep croak on the bassoons is heard as the excitement grows, with the strings sweeping up to another long sustained chord. A stupendous, crashing climax is reached, with brass blaring and fading, and trombones, tubas, and double basses plumbing the depths.

Then, within just four bars, the orchestra subsides from a *fff* fortissimo to a *ppp* pianissimo, and the tempo changes to Andante sostenuto, with a lovely new melody introduced on the strings. An exquisite passage is reached, where the oboes and horns play the melody with an escort of flutes and bassoons. Then, with another change of tempo to *Adagio con moto ed energico* (slow, but with movement and energy), a whirlwind is unleashed on the strings, accompanied by titanic groans on bassoons and tubas. The strings get too excited to run up to another climax, and have to build up to it step by step, with the drums once again breaking through.

A restless heaving, like the folding of sedimentary rocks in the earth's upheaval follows, as the whole orchestra strains and seethes. The Andante melody returns, more beautiful than ever, and more sustained in its climb by the rich trilling of the woodwind above it.

Third movement: Vivacissimo – Lento e suave – Largamente

The scherzo section starts with the strings rushing frantically about on their own, the violins and double basses opening up a vast space between themselves, one scaling the heights, and the other scouring the depths. Flutes and bassoons join in plaintively, and build a climax with all the woodwind playing fortissimo chords. Then the orchestra grows hushed, and in the emptiness a single drum note repeated five times is heard fading to *pppp*. The tempo changes to *Lento e suave* (slow and smooth), and the oboe starts the lovely theme of the trio with the same note repeated nine times, a touch that perhaps only Sibelius could have brought off to such telling effect. The oboes and clarinets play a dialogue over a ground of horns and bassoons. The strings are hushed, apart from a phrase on the viola echoing the repeated notes of the theme. This whole passage is remarkable for its utter simplicity of means.

Trumpets, trombones, and tubas now help to build a climax, and then the strings dash off again with a renewed drive and urgency. Then the horns, with emphatic climbing notes start to build the foundations of the finale, which will follow without a break. The trio section returns, but now the strings begin to transform the repeated stressed notes into a moving line, travelling steadily upwards. The brass builds too. The whole effect is like a giant straining to break his shackles. The struggle is so even that the outcome is delayed by Sibelius with a masterly sense of suspense. But eventually, the theme struggles free, and like a banner that has been waiting to unfurl, the finale unfolds in a blaze of colour.

Fourth movement: Allegro moderato

The strings now sing out the three note, step-like theme, to which the tuba and double basses provide the final flourish. Compare the optimism of this final upward interval with the downward plunge of the big second theme (Example 2) of the

Albrecht Altdorfer 'Die Alexanderschlacht' Archiv für Kunst und Geschichte

The Art Museum of the Ateneum, Helsinki

JEAN SIBELIUS
FINLANDIA
TONDICHTUNG FÜR ORCHESTER

OP. 26 NR. 7

BEARBEITUNG
FÜR PIANOFORTE ZU 2 HÄNDEN

With best wishes to the Mayor New York, Mr. Vincent Impellitteri

Jean Sibelius 1952

Eigentum der Verleger für alle Länder
BREITKOPF & HÄRTEL
LEIPZIG
Für Finnland:
O.Y. Fazern Musikkikauppa, Helsinki
A.B. Fazers Musikhandel, Helsingfors

Sibelius's reputation abroad was assured when Breitkopf and Hartel, the Leipzig publishers, added his name to their catalogue. They issued the very popular Finlandia *(above) as op. 26, no. 7.*

Like Ederfelt's Kaukola *ridge at sunset (left), the peaceful hymn at the heart of* Finlandia *gives us a glimpse of the beauty of Sibelius's beloved country.*

This is a hint of the mighty march theme which Sibelius will oppose to, and eventually unite with the first theme. Clarinets, flutes, and bassoons, continue to build the theme over the perplexed arpeggios of the strings and the reassuring rolls on the drums. As the closing phrases of the theme crash down on trumpets and trombones, and then on the strings, a miracle happens; the lowermost note becomes the beginning of the first theme, climbing up to its development in a lonely woodwind version. The cellos take up this version, and the bassoons oppose with the tailpiece of the march theme. A conflict ensues, in which the simple, uprising faith of the first theme is mocked by the downward cynicism of the march theme in a minor key. But the uprising is successful.

The march theme is won over to the major, and now appears as triumphant as its twin, while woodwind swirl ecstatically above like pennants in the breeze of liberty. Then, no longer in opposition, but beautifully blended, the elemental three-note fragment of the first theme climbs inexorably from the depths of the orchestra to a climax of incredible power and certainty. The confidence in the future that Sibelius expresses in this climactic ending echoes the lines from the *Kalevala:*

I have shown the way to the singers,
Showed the way, and broke the tree-tops,
Cut the branches, shown the pathways.
This way therefore leads the pathway,
Here the path lies newly opened,
Widely open for the singers,

opening movement.

Example 3

con forza

A heraldic optimism is evident in the rhythmic accompaniment on trombones and drums. The second half of the theme is delayed by this magnificent pageantry for some bars, until the strings sing it out, freed of all restraint. They climb higher and higher, inhaling the air of freedom.

A new theme appears on the woodwind, repeated, after a skip of joy, by the strings. This is punctuated, in typical Sibelius fashion, by a loud primeval croak on bassoons and double basses, which then, together with two horns, send the strings off on a windswept search for a new theme. It is the oboes who come up with it first:

Example 4

mp

For the young, who now are growing,
For the rising generation.

Finlandia, op. 26
Programme notes

Finlandia belongs to the same creative period in Sibelius's work as the Second Symphony, and the similarities are apparent from the very opening, with its swelling and fading brass.

After this ceremonial opening, a peaceful hymn is heard on the flutes, oboes and clarinets, with the strings adding their heartfelt agreement. But war breaks out. Fierce fanfares on the brass rattle like gunfire, the tuba and drums roar ominously, and a repressed theme tries to express itself on the strings. The brass section keeps up a covering fire, while the strings advance to storm the heights, which are claimed by a thumping tuba tune with a company of bassoons, drums, cellos, and double basses.

A new section follows, which is really a victory march, in which the triangle plays a conspicuous role. Towards the end, the hymn of peace is heard again and is given space to expand. It leads to a joyful conclusion, with cymbals clashing, and the hymn itself acquires the grandeur of a national anthem.

The final section of **Finlandia** *is a rousing victory march (left), celebrating Finland's freedom from oppression. At the conclusion, the music borders on the bombastic as it assumes the proportions of a national anthem.*

Albert Edenfelt 'March of the Men of Pori'. Gösta Serlachius Museum, Finland

Great interpreters

George Szell (conductor)
Szell was born in Budapest in 1897, though he spent most of his childhood in Vienna. His exceptional pianistic ability was noticed early on and, by the age of ten, he had made his concert début with the Vienna Symphony Orchestra. He completed his studies at the Vienna Academy of Music and later at the Leipzig Academy.

By the age of 17, Szell was appointed assistant at the Berlin Staatsoper under Richard Strauss and, when only 20, he became first conductor at the Strasbourg Municipal Theatre. In 1927, he was appointed musical director of the German Opera House in Prague, where he remained for the next ten years; during this period he also travelled extensively around the world.

After 1937, he joined the Scottish Orchestra but, by chance, was conducting in the US when war broke out. He decided to pursue his career there and, after initial engagements in New York, became the principal conductor of the Metropolitan Opera in 1942. In 1946 he went on to lead the Cleveland Orchestra, a position he held until his death in 1970. His meteoric career in pre-war Europe not withstanding, Szell's reputation rests firmly with his years at the helm of the Cleveland Orchestra. It was his magic and brilliance which raised it to unequalled status in the USA.

Szell's great love was for the Classical and early Romantic period but he was completely at home with such composers as Dvořák, Brahms and Strauss, and greatly admired Sibelius, Bartók and Walton among this century's composers. There is no-one today who would seriously dispute his position as one of the true giants of 20th-century conducting.

Eduard van Beinum (conductor)
Van Beinum was born in Arnhem in 1900 and became a violinist with the Arnhem Orchestra when only 16. After completing his musical studies at the Amsterdam Conservatory, his first venture into conducting was with the Toonkunst Choir at Schiedam in 1921. He stayed with them until 1930, also working as conductor of the Haarlem S.O. (1927–1931).

In 1931, he accepted an invitation to become assistant conductor with the Concertgebouw under Mengelberg. In 1928 he was promoted to the post of principal conductor and, after the war, he became the chief conductor – a position he held until his death in 1959. He toured occasionally, taking the Concertgebouw to the US in 1954 and spending time with the Los Angeles Philharmonic each year after 1956, though based mostly in Amsterdam.

FURTHER LISTENING

Symphony no. 5 in E flat, op. 82
Next to the Second Symphony, the Fifth Symphony is Sibelius's most popular. The work is cast in a heroic mould and is full of vibrant colour and sounds. Indeed, the final version reveals little of the enormous difficulties Sibelius had to surmount in getting the work into its definitive shape: each movement shows a confident progression of ideas, themes and developments, and the musical material is of the highest calibre.

Violin Concerto in D minor, op. 47
This work is one of the most popular violin concertos in the repertoire. It offers plenty of opportunities for the virtuoso performer and is characterized by a wealth of melodic ideas and a rich weave of orchestral textures.

The opening theme is particularly inspired, and if the quality of the music that follows is not always up to the same standard, Sibelius knows how to organize his material so as to have the most effective and powerful impact.

En Saga, op. 9
Sibelius's achievement in the realm of the symphonic poem is outstanding, and works such as *En Saga, Tapiola* and *Luonnotar* give us a wonderful insight into the composer's musical world. *En Saga* is organized along the same lines as a symphony, while at the same time allowing for a greater freedom of poetic fancy. Rich in melodic variety, it displays great tonal flexibility, leaving the listener free to wander off on a musical reverie of his own making.

'Of Gods and Men'

Renewed interest in their cultural heritage of myths and legends provided Scandinavians with a rich source of material which helped promote a profound sense of national pride and identity.

When time began, say the Scandinavian bards, the earth did not exist, nor did the oceans or the sky. Their creation was the starting point of a fantastic mythical world which inspired the early Scandinavian people and which lives on in a rich heritage of myths and legends.

The myths themselves are a unique cultural property. Just as the exploits of the Greek and Roman gods recalled the glories of the classical world to nineteenth-century resistance fighters, so the Scandinavian tradition inspired the northern races and gave them a powerful sense of history and racial identity. It is impossible to exaggerate the relief and pleasure they felt when they found that they too had a dramatic and particular national identity and, to this day, their myths and legends excite profound nationalistic sentiments.

A pre-Christian past

The stories themselves date far back to the long years of the Scandinavian Bronze Age (from about 1600 to 450 BC) and lasted well into the wild, adventurous days of the Vikings. But, as Viking raiding parties swept through western Europe, they came into contact with Christianity and, gradually, its teachings had an effect. Most of Scandinavia was converted to Christianity in the 10th century (though Uppsala in Sweden remained a stubborn outpost for almost 200 years longer) and many of the 'old beliefs' were irrevocably lost.

Archaeology, art and local place names provide scant insight into the early legends, while the writings of early travellers like the Roman historian Tacitus add valuable but limited detail. Other material lies in the Norse sagas and a small collection of Icelandic poems – the *Codex Regius*. Apart from these, the poems and stories gathered together survive almost entirely in manuscripts from later Christian sources.

Heroic inspiration

The central figure of northern legend is Siegfried (Sigurd), who inspired Richard Wagner's supreme operatic cycle, *Der Ring der Nibelungen* and was the hero of the *Volsung Saga* (translated by Eirikr Magnusson and William Morris). This saga was described as the 'Great Story of the North' and stirred fervent patriotism in the souls of many Scandinavians: in Finland, however, a mood of exultant nationalism was aroused by the publication of a quite separate collection – the *Kalevala*. The Kalevala was a collection of Finnish songs with a rich tradition of

myth, magic and folklore (compiled by the scholar, Elias Lönrot) which seemed to compensate for an absence of any other Finnish literature or independent history. History had a hand in its creation, however, for the annexation of Finland by Russia in 1809 led to a reawakening of a national consciousness that found its outlet partly through the burgeoning of Finnish literature. In 1831 *The Society of Finnish Literature* was founded and the pioneering work of a great statesman and national figure, J. V. Snellman (1806–81) gave further impetus to the movement.

Jean Sibelius, Finland's foremost composer, dipped into the Kalevala for inspiration many times: The hero of his first symphony (Kullervo) and Lemminkainen, whose deeds formed the centrepiece of others, were both major characters from its pages. Their appeal, when Finnish autonomy was threatened and the use of the Finnish language was a sensitive political issue, could not be overstated. It

Harald Sohlberg 'Rondane at Night'. National Gallery Oslo/Photo Jacques Lathion

According to Scandinavian legend, there once existed a land of fire in the south and a northern region of ice and snow (above). Sparks of fire slowly thawed the icy floes and, from the vapours, new life was mysteriously formed.

In the epic cycle of myths, the tragic story of Siegfried has achieved wide fame as the basis of Richard Wagner's great opera, The Ring. The adventures and disasters that beset the young hero begin when he slays a huge dragon (left) and so acquires the hoard of gold it protects. Unknown to Siegfried, however, the treasure includes a magic ring that puts a curse on all who possess it.

Archiv für Kunst und Geschichte

was proudly claimed that 'Finland can now say for itself: I too have a history'.

Although of central importance to the Finns, the mythology of the Kalevala was something of a side-show to the sombre tale of doomed gods which formed the theme of the cycle of stories in the rest of Scandinavia. Most of our knowledge of this cycle, which begins with the creation of the world and ends with the fall of the gods and total destruction, comes from poetry written in the tenth century. It is, therefore, closely associated with the Viking Age and its great emphasis on heroic virtue, even though the myths were widespread long before the first Viking ever put to sea. The acceptance of the transience of life and the inevitability of disaster sometimes seems shockingly gloomy, but it gives the gods of that pagan, warlike world an impressive, heroic dignity.

The dawn of time

The cycle begins with the creation of the world: a realm of clouds lay in the north and in the south was a land of fire; between them stood a mighty fountain which gorged out 12 icy rivers. As warm southern winds blew across the ice, droplets of melt water fell and formed the first of all beings – a massive giant.

From this creation, other giants were made but, in their bitter struggle for supremacy, they all but destroyed one another and most were killed. The gods used one of the fallen bodies to create land, mountains, trees and oceans, and the skull of the

One of the most ancient creation myths concerned the great ash tree Yggdrasill (above). Its roots were entwined with serpents, while its massive trunk passed through all the realms of creation.

Odin, was a fearsome Lord of Battle (right). He meted out victory or disaster, stirring up conflict with his huge spear, Gungnir.

Nils Johan Olsson Blommier 'Freyja Seeking her Husband'. Stockholms Universitet

Wielding his mighty hammer and wearing his Belt-of-Strength, Thor (above) was the champion of the gods – supreme in strength and scourge of all their enemies. He was renowned for his quick temper: those who crossed him were likely to have thunderbolts hurled above their heads or find their ships driven toward the rocks as his red beard bristled with anger!

In complete contrast to the awesome power and strength of Odin and Thor, Freyja (above right) was the beautiful and promiscuous goddess of love and fertility. She travelled across the sky in a carriage drawn by cats and lived in a sumptuous banqueting hall where she entertained heroes who had fallen in battle.

giant became the vault of the heavens. From sparks of fire, they then added the moon and galaxies of stars.

Further life was moulded from the rotting flesh of the giant corpse: dwarves were created to live in a subterranean world and, finally, the human race was created from the trunks of trees. Three great gods worked together in making man: Odin gave him breath, Hoenir gave him a soul and the ability to reason and Lodur gave him warmth and colour.

The world the gods created for man and the other beings was made up of nine realms. In the heavenly, upper world, lay three of them: Asgard, where Odin and the gods lived, Vanaheim where the fertility gods lived and Alfheim, the land of the 'light' elves. Below this heavenly strata was the realm of mankind (Midgard), which stood next to the land of the giants (Jotunheim) and was surrounded by a vast ocean, the home of a serpent whose coils encircled the world. Deep in the bowels of this middle level were the realms of the dwarves (Nidavellir) and the 'dark' elves (Swartalfheim). Below them was the home of the dead; a damp, dark place known as Mist-world (Niflheim). Its horrible citadel was presided over by a female monster, Hel. The entrance to the underworld was guarded by a monstrous hound (Garm), whose task it was to prevent any living soul from entering his domain. Growing through all three levels and sheltering all nine realms with its massive branches was the great tree of life, Yggdrasill.

The myths are not absolutely precise about the structure of creation and locations vary from one account to another. The creation part of the myth cycle is largely concerned with natural phenomena: the rainbow was called Bifrost – the fiery bridge between the world of men and the citadel of the gods, while the wind was caused by the wing beats of

Hraesvelg, a giant, corpse-eating eagle. Each part of the cosmos was explained as the result of action by the gods or the giants, and always with sinister reminders of approaching doom. In Asgard (home of the gods), for example, there lay a great plain where the army of gods and men would march out for their last great battle and would suffer defeat at the hands of giants and monsters. Among the halls and palaces of Asgard was Valhalla, where great heroes from the world of man, saved from Hel, waited for the day when they would fight alongside the gods. But however many they numbered and however heroically they fought, they were all destined to fail.

The pantheon of gods

The world painted in Scandinavian myth carries the seeds of its own destruction: but the day of Doom (Ragnarok) lies in the future. Before it dawned there would be a cycle of clashes between gods and giants which illustrated the powers and place of each god in the pantheon. Odin was the greatest of them all and, to some extent, was their ruler. But he was not the strongest or even the most trustworthy. He had powers to change shape and could oversee every action in all nine worlds when he sat upon his magic throne. He was immensely wise, but had made great personal sacrifices to gain this wisdom. He was one eyed, because he had given up an eye as a pledge when he drank from the Spring of Mimir, source of all wisdom. He even hanged himself in the tree of life in order to learn the knowledge of the dead. He loved warfare and was the god of battle. He decided which side would win – but his decision-making was capricious and he liked to stir up trouble. Finally, he had the gift of poetry and, like the ancient Greek gods, was a determined seducer (even raper) of

Ferdinand Leeke 'La Walkyrie'/Edimedea

women.

Next to Odin in importance was his son Thor, who was a far more straightforward and better liked divinity. He was the strongest god — matchlessly strong — somewhat slow-witted but quick-tempered and with a vast, earthy appetite. He was the guardian of men and gods and constantly called upon to battle to the death with awesome giants – killing them with his indestructible hammer. Emotionally, he was the god of order, keeping the forces of chaos at bay and the myths made it clear that, if his strength was ever overcome by magic or if he lost the magic hammer, the giants would lose no time in storming Asgard and overrunning the world of men.

Among the fertility gods, the most important were Njord, guardian of ships and seafarers, and his two children, Freyr, god of plenty, and Freyja, most beautiful of the goddesses. Freyja plays quite a leading part in the myths, being portrayed as desirable and promiscuous – a goddess of battle as well as love.

Other deities in the pantheon included Tyr, bravest of all. He was the only god prepared to sacrifice his own hand so that a huge wolf could be captured. In the tale, the wolf had grown so strong and vicious that the gods feared for their own safety. They obtained magically strong but flimsy-looking chains (made by the dwarves) and cunningly challenged the wolf to prove his strength by being bound and then bursting his shackles. The wolf, however, was suspicious and demanded that one of the gods put a hand in his mouth as a surety that they would release him if his strength failed. Only Tyr was prepared to lose his hand as the price for capturing

Closely associated with Odin were the Valkyries (left), helmeted goddesses who carried slain warriors to the land of the gods. Astride flying steeds with dew and hailstones dripping from their manes, the Valkyries also had the power to transform themselves into gentle and graceful swan maidens. Among their number was the beautiful Brunnhilde (above), who thwarted Odin and, despite her desperate pleading, was stripped of her divine powers and condemned to live in the land of men. Lying in a magically induced slumber, she could only be saved by a hero who dared to ride through the ring of flames that encircled her. Such a hero finally came – and was none other than Siegfried.

the beast and he bravely volunteered.

Another of the more important gods was Heimdall, a sleepless watchman who would summon the host of Asgard on his horn when the day of reckoning approached. Most important of all was Heimdall's particular enemy, the treacherous, cunning, dynamic mixture of god and devil, Loki (he would lead the side of the the giants and monsters in their final battle). Although he was descended from giants, Loki appeared to be one of the gods and spent much of his time at Asgard. He was amusing and clever, the chosen companion of both Odin and Thor, but his nature was flawed. Too tricky for his own good, his many pranks often went sour and he nursed a growing hatred and resentment of those more powerful or popular than himself. It was this resentment that finally led him to commit the unforgivable crime of murdering one of the gods.

The enemy within

An early story illustrates perfectly how much Loki was identified with the gods and how far his sharp wits could cause them trouble. During one of the many battles against the giants, the walls of Asgard had been ruined and the task of rebuilding them was so great that they had been left unrepaired. One day a solitary horseman cantered over the rainbow bridge and offered to build impregnable walls around the entire citadel – in less than eighteen months. In exchange for this, he wanted the sun, the moon and the goddess Freyja.

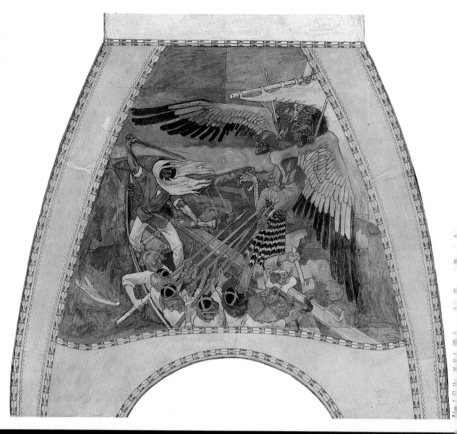

One of the liveliest heroes of the Kalevala is Lemminkainen, a debonair but reckless young man. To prove himself to his future bride, he is ordered to kill a particular swan but is betrayed by an old man. His body is torn to pieces and thrown into the river. But his enemy has reckoned without the magical powers of the hero's mother. Using her black arts, she rebuilds the lifeless body (right). She then enlists the help of a bee to bring her honey from beyond 'the highest heaven'. Anointed with this potent balm, Lemminkainen is finally revived.

Akseli Gallen-Kallela 'Lammin Käinen's Mother' The Art Museum of the Ateneum, Helsinki

Full of strange and mystical events, one of the central stories in the Kalevala concerns the theft of a magic talisman, the sampo, crafted by the blacksmith (Ilmarinen) as a gift to his wife's family. The talisman proves to have great power and, after his wife's death, Ilmarinen and two friends resolve to steal it. Before the heroes can escape with their prize, however, they must fend off the fierce attacks of its rightful owners (left).

Kullervo (right) was one of the key figures in the Finnish sagas. He was an immensely strong but very bad-natured warrior who used his gifts for evil ends.

The gods at first rejected the offer outright, but Loki suggested that they agree to the price on condition that the work was completed within six months. His idea was that such a task would prove impossible but much of the work would be done and the gods would not be obliged to pay out anything. With some hesitation, the mysterious mason agreed to the terms, but only if he was allowed the help of his stallion. Loki eagerly pressed the case and the bargain was struck.

The stallion, however, turned out to be a trump card, hauling huge loads of rock for the tireless stranger to use. At this point, he was identified as a giant – a scheming enemy – and, worse still, he was working fast enough to win the prize. The gods were horrified to think that they would be deprived of light and warmth when they paid out with the sun and moon, and Freyja wept bitterly at the thought of being carried away to the land of the giants. Furiously, the gods rounded on Loki and made him swear to make the giant lose the wager. Just before completion of the wall, Loki changed himself into a mare and enticed the stallion away, so winning the day.

But the story does not end there. Knowing that he had failed, the giant threatened the gods with force and demanded his reward regardless. They had the good sense to send for Thor, however, who came running, eager for the fight and characteristically despatched the giant with one mighty blow of his hammer. As a postscript to the episode, Loki returned some months later, leading an eight-legged grey horse which he presented to Odin. He claimed to have conceived the horse by the giant's stallion, and said that no other steed could match his extraordinary offspring for pace.

The tale is impressively complete in its detail of the relationship between the various gods and in stressing the constant threat presented by the giants. It also makes the disturbing point that Loki was capable of changing sex as well as shape, and of bearing children as well as fathering them! By one means or another, this resulted in his having numerous progeny, including three of the vilest and most deadly monsters in creation: Hel, the rotting hag who owned the citadel of the dead; the wolf who had bitten off Tyr's hand (and was destined, one day, to kill Odin) and the giant serpent who encircled the world of men. It was this serpent who would confront Thor in the final battle, being crushed by his hammer blows but, in its death throes, spewing out venom that would kill Thor as well.

The story of the rebuilding of the walls of Asgard is only one of many myths which form a linked chain describing a system of religious beliefs but also warning of coming destruction. In many of the tales, the threat to the gods is only just averted. Their great weakness is that they are not immortal – they can be maimed or killed.

The gathering gloom

As the cycle proceeds, the shadows darken and Valhalla fills with heroes preparing for the final battle. A belief in fate pervades the religious message of the myths. When a man was born, his fate was decided and was inescapable. All he could hope to do was to choose the manner in which he met his end – bravely or otherwise. There is great stress laid on courage and strength: the best fate that could befall a man was to fall heroically in battle and so be borne to Asgard by the Valkyries – Odin's beautiful shield maidens – and to feast in Valhalla till Doomsday.

Just as men were fated, so were the gods. As time passed, Loki had changed from a slightly malicious joker to a bitter, tormented demon who was wildly resentful of those around him. Among the gods, the wisest and most beautiful was Balder, the son of Odin – a god whose sweet disposition made him universally

R. W. Ekman 'Kreet Haapasalo Playing the Kantale'. The Art Museum of the Ateneum, Helsinki

loved. Balder became wracked by frightening dreams that foretold his death and deeply alarmed the other gods. In a desperate attempt to forestall his fate, his mother visited everything in the nine worlds wringing out the promise that it would not harm him. Every animal, every plant, every stone and every illness promised in turn not to hurt the beloved god. When all the pledges were made, Asgard sighed with relief and the gods began a celebratory game of hurling rocks and weapons at Balder to watch them turn away from him and leave him unscathed.

Loki, however, found out that one object – the humble mistletoe – had been overlooked and he proceeded to fashion a deadly dart from its growth. Ever treacherous, he then went to Balder's blind brother, placed the mistletoe dart in his hand and urged him to join the sport by throwing it. Innocently the brother agreed and, with a single blow of the dart, Balder was struck dead. Amid the ensuing pandemonium, the distraught mother pleaded for a volunteer to go to the underworld and ask Hel to release Balder. One of the dead god's brothers volunteered and, after a horrifying journey, he persuaded Hel to agree – but she stipulated that everything in creation must first weep for the slain god. Once again the mother did her rounds and everything agreed to the condition. But it was to no avail! Loki, in the form of giantess, refused to weep and professed complete contempt for Balder.

After a rancorous argument with the other gods, Loki fled but was tracked down and made to face a severe punishment for his crimes. He was bound, face upwards, in a gloomy cave while a serpent dripped venom into his face. His faithful wife held a bowl over him to catch the stream of venom but, every time she turned to empty the bowl, the drip of stinging poison made Loki writhe in agony.

At this stage, the myth cycle had dealt solely with the past deeds of the gods but then it moves into the 'present' and a short period during which the gods still rule in Asgard. The last story, however, is a prophecy of coming doom. The earth will be wracked by wars and crimes and gripped by a bone-chilling cold spell of three terrible winters with no summer between them. The ground will shake and all bonds and fetters will burst, freeing Loki and the great wolf so that they can take part in the final battle. The end of each of the principal gods is described in a series of duels with terrible monsters and the heroes who march out of Valhalla in 540 columns of 800 men, are all destined to be killed in battle. The flaming sword of the giant Surt will set all creation on fire and the earth will sink below the sea. Following this titanic conclusion, the prophecy makes an unconvincing effort to foretell rebirth: a green earth will rise again from the sea, some of the minor gods will have survived and a man and woman will have hidden from destruction in the branches of the tree of life.

The idea of total and final destruction was perhaps, too much to bear and a message of hope was tacked on to the main body of stories. In a way, this contradicts the central theme of the myth cycle, which is one of the inevitability of fate. It makes a stirring and tragic tale, an epic in praise of courage and the defiance of a grim destiny and a message that inspired nationalists of a later age.

National Museum of Finland, Helsinki

Kalewala

(aiffa

Wanhoja Karjalan Runoja

Suomen kanfan muinofista ajoista.

1. Ofa.

Helfingisfä, 1835.
Präntätty J. C. Frenckellin ja Pojan tykönä.

The Kalevala was not one complete written saga, but a collection of old Finnish ballads, songs and folklore handed down by word of mouth from one generation to the next (top). It was gathered together and first published as a single, epic story in 1835 (above).

The Kalevala

The great myth cycle was not the only religious tradition in Scandinavia. Co-existing with it was a definitively Finnish collection of songs and stories that told a similarly robust but less gloomy tale of creation and magical adventure. The proponents were not gods – indeed they frequently prayed to a god who was somewhat like Thor in character – nor were they simply men who had the gift of magic. They were more nearly concepts that had been given personalities. The chief of them, Vainamoinen, for example, was the embodiment of wisdom, poetry and endeavour. His companion (Ilmarinen) was the archetypal craftsman, while another, Lemminkainen, was the soul of rashness and charm.

Their adventures, and many other pieces of folklore, were recorded in song. They are described as the people of a district called Kalevala and they are in frequent dispute with a neighbouring district, North Farm. North Farm itself appears to have been an immensely rich Viking Age-farm which suffered from the to-ing and fro-ing of the mythical Finnish heroes as they came to wage war, woo the daughter of its chieftain or pursue other ends. The purpose and origin of the tales is now rather obscure – but its importance to the Finnish people is paramount.

The songs were collected in the middle of the last century and have always had immense appeal to the national sentiments of the Finns – the name Kalevala is a poetic name for Finland and means 'Land of Heroes'. Apart from being in the Finnish language and telling tales of Finnish characters, they are entertaining and well composed. Almost every line spoken by the devil-may-care Lemminkainen, for instance, is redolent of his attitude to life. When he sets off to attend a wedding at North Farm, he dismisses complaints that he has not even been invited: 'Wretched people go by invitation, a good man skips along without one'. When this carefree adventurer arrives at the wedding, he behaves so badly that he provokes the master of the farm to a duel and then kills him. Lemminkainen flees from vengeance and lands up in a remote island where, true to his reputation as a charmer of women, he seduces so many of the girls that he once again has to flee – this time from their outraged fathers and husbands. He is the eternal, entertaining rogue.

Not all the tales are so full of zest and humour. There is also a sullen, tragic character who murders a friend's wife, seduces his own sister in a ghastly episode of mistaken identity and ends by committing suicide. Taken together, the stories are the great Finnish national epic and yet they have more to offer besides: they also contain much folklore on bridal songs, farming lays and hunting charms which are invaluable parts of Finnish history. Though many of its key elements are no longer of any practical significance to Finnish people – the Kalevala is more than anything else, a sequence of poetry with magical and ritual incantations that give power over nature – the stories are richly detailed and enjoyable in their own right and, most importantly, they are a source of national inspiration to the Finns. The stirring epic fired the imaginations of one of Finland's greatest artists, Akseli Gallen-Kallela (1865–1931), her greatest musician, Jean Sibelius and, indirectly, the distinguished poet Eino Leino. Translated into 20 languages – the distinctive metre was even imitated by Longfellow in his North American epic, Hiawatha – its powerful appeal has extended far beyond the national boundaries of Finland and, like the main body of Scandinavian mythology, has provided pleasure and entertainment to people around the world.

Following her long years of acquiescence to Swedish domination, Finland seemed to awake with a start of national awareness after her annexation by Russia in 1809. This new awareness led to the founding of a Society of Finnish Literature (left) – an institution which played a significant role in raising the status of Finnish as a language of equal importance to Swedish: it was in this atmosphere of renewed pride and consciousness that the Kalevala was published.

Contemporary composers

Ferruccio Busoni (1866-1924)

A brilliant pianist and a noted composer, Busoni was encouraged to take up music by his parents, both musicians. He studied in Vienna and Leipzig, and later held teaching posts all over the world, including Helsinki, Moscow and Boston. In 1894, he settled in Berlin. He became known for transcribing and arranging the works of Bach and Liszt, and for his skill as a pianist. He also organized several concerts featuring the works of contemporary composers. His own eclectic works included many piano pieces, works for orchestra with piano, and three operas, including *Doctor Faust* (completed by his pupil Philipp Jarnach in 1925).

Niels Gade (1817-1890)

The founder of the romantic nationalist movement in Danish music, Gade was born in Copenhagen and studied violin and composition there. Mendelssohn was an early supporter of his works, conducting his first symphony in Leipzig in 1843. Gade's international reputation was further enhanced after Schumann praised the Scandinavian character of his works in a music journal. His works, including overtures, symphonies and ballet scores, reflected the spirit of Danish folk music.

Louis Moreau Gottschalk (1829-1869)

Born in New Orleans of English-Jewish and French-Creole parents, Gottschalk was only 13 when he left Louisiana for Paris to study music. After several years of European concert tours, he returned to America in 1853 as a concert pianist. He toured North and South America extensively with his romantic and sentimental piano compositions. His works showed a variety of influences, including the Creole folk music of his birthplace; his constant touring made him the first internationally famous American composer.

Victor Herbert (1859-1924)

Born in Ireland and trained as a cello player in Germany, Herbert moved to the United States in 1886 to join the Metropolitan Opera as a cellist. He eventually became an American citizen, but his compositional work reflected his grounding in the European tradition. Herbert served as principal conductor of the Pittsburgh Symphony Orchestra (1898-1904); in later years, he gave up conducting to compose a number of popular operettas including *Babes in Toyland* (1903). He was the first American to write an original score for a motion picture in 1916 for *The Fall of a Nation.*

Charles Ives (1874-1954)

One of the greatest American experimental composers, Ives actually made his career in insurance, composing only in the evenings and on weekends and holidays. During this limited time, however, the native New Englander composed more than 150 works. He first gained attention in the early 1940s with his works for piano, which drew upon American themes in an unconventional and highly imaginative style. He also composed symphonies, chamber works and choral pieces. He remained relatively unknown for most of his life, but during his last years gained a following as a musical pioneer.

Leoš Janáček (1854-1928)

Born in Czechoslovakia, Janáček trained as a schoolmaster in Brno and first gained notice as a composer of choral works. Perhaps as a result of his father's Moravian background, he began collecting Moravian folk songs in 1885 and his music reflected their influence. *Jenufa*, his opera set in a Moravian village, firmly established his reputation in a 1916 performance in Prague. He continued to develop his highly personal and intense style of composition in a series of successful operas written in the mid-1920s.

John Phillip Sousa (1854-1932)

Although Sousa wrote many kinds of music, he is most remembered for his marches. Born in Washington, D.C., he studied violin as a young man and played in several theatre orchestras. He formed his own band in 1892 and toured throughout the world with his own compositions and a selection of light classical works. His famous marches are bold and melodic, showing his special ear for understanding a band's sound. The sousaphone, a tuba designed for marching bands, was named in his honour.

Bibliography

Abraham, G. *Grieg: A Symposium.* Littlefield (Totowa, 1975).

Abraham, G. *The Music of Sibelius.* Da Capo (New York, 1975).

Butterworth, N. *Dvořák: His Life and Times.* Paganiniana (Neptune, 1981).

Clapham, J. *Antonín Dvořák: Musician and Craftsman.* Hyperion (Westport, 1966).

Clapham, J. *Dvořák.* Norton (New York, 1979).

Clapham, J. *Smetana.* J. M. Dent (London, 1962).

Gray, C. *Jean Sibelius.* Hyperion (Westport, 1979).

Horton, J. *Grieg.* Littlefield (Totowa, 1975).

Horton, J. *Scandinavian Music: A Short History.* Greenwood (Westport, 1975).

Large, B. *Smetana.* Da Capo (New York, 1985).

Layton, R. *Dvořák Symphonies and Concertos.* University of Washington Press (Seattle, 1978).

Layton, R. *Sibelius.* Rowman (Totowa, 1984).

Tawastsjerna, E. *Sibelius.* English trans. University of California Press (Berkeley, 1976).

Index